Socializing

MARK ELLIS AND NINA O'DRISCOLL

Longman

SERIES EDITOR NINA O'DRISCOLL
WITH MARK ELLIS AND ADRIAN PILBEAM

The authors work for Language Training Services

Longman Group UK Limited,
Longman House, Burnt Mill, Harlow
Essex CM20 2JE, England
and Associated Companies throughout the world

© Mark Ellis, Nina O'Driscoll and Adrian Pilbeam 1987
Published jointly by Studentlitteratur AB, Lund, Sweden
and Longman Group UK Limited, London, England.

First published 1987
Third impression 1989
First published in colour 1992

ISBN 0 582 09308 2

Set in 9/11pt Linotron 202 Helvetica

Produced by Longman Group (FE) Ltd
Printed in Hong Kong

Acknowledgements

We are grateful to the following for their permission to
reproduce copyright photographs:

Ace Photo Agency for page 56; The Image Bank for pages
24 and 33; Tony Stone Worldwide for pages 6 and 41;
The Telegraph Colour Library for page 48; Zefa Picture
Library (UK) Limited for page 15.

Cover Photograph by Tony Stone Worldwide.

Contents

Introduction   4

1   Introductions   6

2   Greetings   15

3   Concluding a conversation   24

4   Inviting   33

5   Thanking and showing appreciation   41

6   Offering and requesting   48

7   The first five minutes   56

Key   63

INTRODUCTION TO THE LEARNER

Socializing is part of the Longman Business Skills series. It presents and practises the language used in a variety of typical social situations – situations which professional people are likely to meet while travelling abroad on business, receiving visitors in their workplace or working on a day to day basis in an international enviroment.

Objectives The material is designed to help you focus directly on the language used in social exchanges by providing short model conversations which include appropriate expressions and phrases.

It also gives you practice in using some of these expressions yourself, and makes it easier for you to judge whether a situation demands a friendly 'informal' style or something safer and more 'neutral'.

The material The material is based around an audio cassette. This should be used in conjunction with the book. The material is designed for use on your own or in class and assumes that you have at least a basic general knowledge of English.

The book The book consists of seven units. The first six are the main units and concentrate on special areas of language, e.g. *Greetings* in Unit 2 and *Inviting* in Unit 4. Unit 7 – *The first five minutes* – is designed as a review unit, but also looks at ways of starting up and developing conversations.

The cassette The cassette contains the short model dialogues which illustrate the main language points in the units. You will hear examples of social exhanges where people obviously know each other well and use 'informal' language, and examples where people have just met or know each other only at a business level and use 'neutral' language. There are no examples of very informal or formal social exchanges.

The cassette also contains cues to many of the Language Practices. If you are using this book by yourself, try to record your responses to these cues or, if this is difficult, say them aloud and then write them down so you can compare them with the answers in the key.

Using the material Each unit is divided into two *separate* but related parts. For example, if you look at Unit 1, you will see that the first part looks at different ways of introducing yourself, while part two looks at ways of introducing others.

Each part of a unit contains the following steps. You should work through them in order.

BACKGROUND Read this to establish the context for the main listening component.

COMPREHENSION CHECK AND FOCUS ON LANGUAGE This involves listening to two or three short dialogues, first for general comprehension and then again to focus on the actual expressions and phrases being used.

LANGUAGE SUMMARY Each unit contains several of these. They provide a short account of the key language points and are designed as reference material.

PRACTICE This includes various activities designed to help you use the expressions and phrases presented in the Dialogues and Language Summaries.

The Key The key contains the tapescripts and answers to all the activities in a unit. In many of the Practices a suggested answer has been given. These should not be seen as the only correct answer, but more as models of what people *could* say in the situation.

1

Introductions

PART 1   INTRODUCING YOURSELF

Background   Guy Giradeaux works in the export division of Le Saucier, a French company producing kitchen appliances and equipment.

His work frequently takes him on business outside France.

Comprehension Check   Listen to the three dialogues which take place while Guy is on one of these trips, and answer the questions.

1 Has he met any of the people he is speaking to before?

2 In which dialogue is Guy talking to

    a a colleague in one of the subsidiaries?
    b a security guard?
    c a customer?

3 Which of the three dialogues is

    a friendly and informal?
    b neutral and polite?
    c impersonal and official?

> Check your answers in the key.

Focus on Language   Listen to each of the dialogues again and complete the missing parts of the extracts, following the notes on the right. Then do the tasks that follow.

DIALOGUE 1   The style is **neutral**.

NOTES

Guard   _____   Greets him.

Guy   *Good morning.* _____ *Guy Giradeaux.* _____ *Mr Binder at ten.*

Greets him and identifies himself. Explains the purpose of the visit.

Guard   *Mr Binder. Sales Department?*

Guy   *That's right.*

Guard   _____ *name* _____?   Checks his name.

Guy   *Guy Giradeaux.*

Guard   *Okay, I'll. . .*

Tasks   **a** Which of the three phrases could Guy also use to introduce himself in this situation?

    I'm. . .
    I'm called. . .
    Let me introduce myself.

b What other phrase could be used to explain the purpose of Guy's visit? Make a sentence using *I/here/see/Mr Binder.*

DIALOGUE 2   The style is **neutral.**

Margareta   _____ ?   _____ *Margareta Sandström.*

_____ *sales over here in the Stockholm area.*

Guy   *How do you do, Mrs Sandström?* _____ .

Margareta   *Nice to meet you too. . .*

NOTES

Greets him and identifies herself.

Adds some more details about herself.

Returns the greeting.

Tasks   **a** Complete the other phrases below which Margareta could also use in this situation:

to identify herself
    My. . .

to talk about her responsibilities
    I'm in charge of. . .

b Which of the three sentences could Guy also use to introduce himself in this situation?

I'm delighted to see you.
Great to meet you.
I'm very pleased to meet you.

DIALOGUE 3   The style is **informal.**

David   *Mr Giradeaux?*

Guy   *Yes, that's right, Guy Giradeaux.*

David   _____ , *Guy,* _____ *David Fairlawn. Welcome to Daylight Electrics.* _____ .

Guy   _____ , *David.* _____ .

David   *Did you. . .*

NOTES

Checks the visitor's identity.

Greets the visitor, and introduces himself.

Returns the greeting.

Tasks   Which of these phrases could also be used in this situation:

a to check the identity of the visitor?

You're Mr Giradeaux, aren't you?
Are you Mr Giradeaux?
Are you Mr Giradeaux by any chance?

b to return the greeting?

> *How do you do, Mr Fairlawn. I'm very pleased to be here.*
> *Good to see you, David.*
> *Hello, David. Nice to meet you.*

Check your answers in the key.

Language Summary

Identifying yourself

When you identify yourself to someone you often need to give not only your name, but also any other relevant details about yourself or the situation.

Identification	Relevant information
Hello, I'm. . .	*from. . .*
Hello, my name is. . .	*I work for. . .*
Hello, let me introduce myself,	*I'm in charge of. . .*
I'm . . .	*I'm responsible for. . .*
Hello, first name + surname	*I've got an appointment with. . .*

PRACTICE 1

What would you say to identify yourself in the following situations?

EXAMPLE

You have arrived at a hotel where you have a reservation for tonight and tomorrow night.

Good _____ *evening.*
My name _____ *is Paul Daniels. I have a*
room booked _____ *for tonight and tomorrow night.*

a You work for a company called Databloc and have just arrived at a company you are visiting. You have an appointment with Mr Bell, Personnel Department, at 10.30. The first person you see is the security guard.

Hello, _____
from _____ .
I've _____ .

b The security guard has now directed you to Mr Bell's office where his secretary is waiting for you. You introduce yourself.

Hello, _____ .

c You have been asked to look after a visitor who has come to see a colleague of yours. Introduce yourself and explain what you do in the company.

Hello, let _____ .
I'm _____ .

d You are meeting a Japanese visitor, Mr Yamamoto at the airport. He is going to spend a couple of days in your company. Identify yourself and your company.

Hello, _____

from _____ .

I'm _____ .

> Check your answers in the key.

Language Summary

Greetings for first meetings

When you meet people for the first time on a personal or business basis it's usual to shake hands. This is when the greeting phrase *How do you do?* is appropriate, but it is **only** used on **first** meetings.

First greeting	
NEUTRAL	
How do you do?	*I'm (very) pleased/delighted to meet you.*
	It's (very) nice to meet you.
INFORMAL	
How do you do?	*Nice/good to meet you.*
Hello.	*Nice to have you with us.*
Hi. (very informal but more frequent in American English)	*Pleased to meet you.*
Reply to the greeting	
NEUTRAL	
How do you do?	*It's (very) nice to meet you too.*
	I'm pleased to meet you too.
INFORMAL	
How do you do?	*Nice/good to meet you too.*
Hello.	*Pleased to meet you too.*
Hi. (very informal)	

PRACTICE 2   Decide how you would greet people in the following five situations. Match the greeting on the right with the situation on the left.

SITUATION

GREETING

a You have been in correspondence ➤ *It's nice to put a face to a name.* with someone for some time. Finally you meet face to face.

b You have had appointments with this person on two or three occasions, but something has always gone wrong. Finally you meet.

We're very pleased to have you with us.

c Someone has just arrived in your company to spend six months doing some computer training.

I'm very pleased to welcome you all here.

d A trade delegation from Japan is visiting your company.

I'm pleased to meet you.

e You are meeting your counterpart in another subsidiary.

It's very nice to meet you at last.

PRACTICE 3 Reorganize the numbered phrases below as dialogues. Indicate the correct sequence and order of the speakers.

Speakers

Donald and Janine

Dialogue A

1 *Pleased to meet you too.*
2 *You must be Janine Brown.*
3 *Hello, I'm Donald Flinders. I'm pleased to meet you.*
4 *Yes, that's right.*

Speakers

Mr Smallbone and
Mr Francis

Dialogue B

1 *Yes, that's me.*
2 *Are you Mr Francis, by any chance?*
3 *Nice to meet you.*
4 *I'm Head of Marketing here. You're from Databloc, aren't you?*
5 *I'm Clive Smallbone.*
6 *Yes, that's right.*

Check your answers in the key.

PART 2 INTRODUCING OTHERS

Background Terry Finnigan works for an Irish ship-building company in their Sales Department.

Comprehension Check Listen to the three short dialogues in which he introduces visitors to various colleagues.

1 Which of the conversations takes place

  a at a party?
  b before a meeting?
  c in someone's office?

2 What information does Terry give about each of the visitors before or during the introduction?

Ivan Chekov   **a** _____

                        b _____

Wolfgang Jaeger   _____

John Benny   **a** _____

                        b _____

                        c _____

> Check your answers in the key.

Focus on Language

Listen to the dialogues again and complete the missing parts of the extracts, following the notes on the right. Then do the tasks that follow.

DIALOGUE 4   The style is **neutral.**

          NOTES

Terry   _Georgina, _____ Ivan Chekov, the head of the Russian Trade Delegation, _____?_

     Checks to see if the visitor is known.

Georgina   _No, not yet._

Terry   _Well, come over and _____. Interesting man. . ._

     Offers an introduction.

     . . .

Terry   _Hello, Mr Chekov. I hope you're enjoying the party._

Mr Chekov   _Yes, very much._

Terry   _Mr Chekov, _____ a colleague of mine, Georgina Smiles from the design team._

     Introduces the two people.

Mr Chekov   _How do you do?_

     They greet each other.

Georgina   _How do you do? _____, Mr Chekov._

Task   Which of these two sentences could also be used to introduce someone in this situation?

May I introduce a colleague of mine?
I want you to meet a colleague.

DIALOGUE 5   The style is **informal.**

          NOTES

Terry   _Hello, Patrick. If you've got a minute, _____

     Offers to introduce the visitor.

Patrick   _Certainly. Come in, I'll be with you in a moment. Right._

Terry   _Patrick, _____ Wolfgang Jaeger from Deutsche Lloyd. Patrick O'Connor, our Export Manager._

     Introduces the two men.

Patrick   _____, Wolfgang. Nice _____ us._

     They greet each other.

Wolfgang   _How do you do?_

Task   The two phrases below can also be used to introduce people.
Which one is not appropriate in this context?

I'd like to present to you. . .
May I introduce. . .?

DIALOGUE 6   The style is **neutral**.

NOTES

Terry   *Well, if everybody's here, let's begin. First of all, _____ John Benny from the Chicago Consulting Group. . .*

Welcomes the visitor.

John, _____ my colleagues from left to right, James O'Driscoll from R and D. . .

Introduces the visitor to the group.

Task   What other phrase could be used for the introduction? Begin your introduction with *I'd. . .my colleagues.*

> Check your
> answers in the key.

Language Summary

Introducing people

When introducing people it is often necessary to give not only their names but also other relevant information, e.g. nationality, company, department, job, etc.

Phrase of introduction		+	relevant information
NEUTRAL			
Mr Jaeger	I'd like you to meet	Claude René	a colleague of mine from France.
	May I introduce		
	I'd like to introduce		our Marketing Manager.
INFORMAL			
Wolfgang	Can I introduce	John Benny	He's with the Chicago Consulting Group.
	This is		a friend of mine.
	I want you to meet		He's over here on business.

PRACTICE 4   Christopher Hutton has recently joined your company. How would you introduce the following people to him?

EXAMPLE
This   is Paula Brown my secetary

a *I'd* _____

b *I want* _____

c *May* _____

Name	Nationality	Company	Job	Style for introduction
Paula Brown		Same company as you	Your secretary	Informal business context
a Tom de Wey	Dutch	Same company Dutch subsidiary	Marketing Manager	Rather formal business context
b Francis Renard	French		A friend	Informal social context
c Mr Utowa	Japanese		Sales Manager of a supplier	Formal context

PRACTICE 5 Read the situation outlined below. Then complete the missing part of the dialogue, following the notes on the right.

Rita Vanders works for a Dutch company, OMU, in the Sales Department. She is visiting a British supplier. Her contact there is David Thompson, they have met before and know each other quite well.

NOTES

Rita *Hello, David. _____?*

Greets him and makes an enquiry.

David *Fine, and you?*

Replies.

Rita *Very well, actually.*

Replies.

David _____

Checks to make sure Rita hasn't met his new assistant Peter Jennings.

Rita *No, we haven't met.*

David *Peter, _____ Rita Vanders from OMU in Holland.*

Introduces Rita to Peter.

PRACTICE 6 Listen to the cassette. You have invited a foreign guest, John Taylor, to your home for dinner. John is a regular visitor from your company's English subsidiary. You will hear three different instructions asking you to introduce him to various people. Stop the cassette after each instruction and make your response. You will hear a suggested answer after a pause.

Check your answers in the key.

2

Greetings

Aims This unit shows you how to
- greet people you see frequently
- greet people you see from time to time
- respond to greetings

PART 1   DAILY GREETINGS

Background   David Hamilton works at the European HQ of an American multi-national, ATI. The headquarters are in Brussels.

Comprehension Check   Listen to the three short dialogues in which David Hamilton greets three people who work in the same department as he does. Answer the questions.

1 In which dialogue is he greeting

  a a fellow manager?
  b his assistant?
  c his secretary?

2 In which dialogue is he greeting someone he has not seen for some weeks?

3 Which of these descriptions best describes David Hamilton's relationship with the people he works with?

  a relaxed and friendly
  b formal

4 In which of the dialogues is David Hamilton addressed by his title and surname?

> Check your answers in the key.

Focus on Language   Listen to the dialogues again and complete the missing parts of the extracts, following the notes on the right. Then do the tasks that follow.

DIALOGUE 1   The style is **neutral.**

		NOTES
Tom	_____, Mr Hamilton.	Greets him.
David	_____, Tom. _____?	Greets him with a general enquiry about the office.
Tom	_____. By the way, I've. . .	Reply to the enquiry.

Task   Which of the three questions below could David Hamilton also use to make his general enquiry about the office?

How's it going?   Are you okay?   How are you?

DIALOGUE 2   The style is **neutral.**

		NOTES
David	*Morning, Isabel. _____?*	Greets her with personal enquiry.
Isabel	*Oh, _____, Mr Hamilton. _____. Terrible morning, isn't it?*	Greets him and replies to the enquiry.
David	*Yes, ...*	

Task Which of the two phrases below could David Hamilton also use to greet Isabel?

Are you all right?   Is everything all right?

DIALOGUE 3 The style is **informal.**

		NOTES
David	*Morning, Jane. You're in early. _____ the holiday?*	Greets her with a specific enquiry.
Jane	*Oh, hello, David. Holiday? Just look at all this, it'll take days to work through. No really, David, _____ Just what I needed.*	Replies to the enquiry.
David	*Sounds great.*	
Jane	*_____ here?*	General enquiry about the office.
David	*_____ . By the way, there's a . . .*	Replies to this enquiry.

Tasks

a What other phrase could be used to enquire about the holiday? Make a sentence using *How/you/enjoy/holiday.*

b Jane's reply to the enquiry was very positive. What other words could she use? Choose from *nice/marvellous/good/fine.*

Check your
answers in the key.

Language Summary

Daily greetings

When greeting people, the greeting is often combined with some form of *enquiry* about the person or situation.

Greeting	Follow-up enquiry	Reply
Hello.	*How are you?*	*Very well, thanks.*
Hi.	*How are you doing?*	
(Good) morning.	*How are things? have things been?*	*Not too bad.*
(Good) afternoon.	*Is everything okay/ all right?*	*Fine, thank you.*

In extract three David Hamilton combines his greeting with a *specific enquiry* about the other speaker's holiday.

These more specific enquiries are appropriate if you know something specific about the person you are greeting. They often begin with the question word *How*, e.g. *How was your holiday?*

Greeting	Specific enquiry	Reply
Hello.	*How was your holiday?*	*Very good.*
Hi.	*How was the trip?*	*Very interesting.*
(Good) morning.	*How did the meeting go?* *How did you enjoy* *the film?*	*Very well/fine.* *Very much.*

PRACTICE 1 What would you say if you were greeting people in the following situations? Begin each of your specific enquiries with *How*.

a You are meeting a friend at the airport. He's just come through customs.

b A friend of yours went to see a film on your recommendation.

c A colleague of yours has just got back from an overseas business trip.

d The wife of a friend of yours has had to go into hospital – you know them both very well.

e You are greeting a friend who has just changed job. You have not seen him or her since this happened.

PRACTICE 2 Decide on the most appropriate greeting in each of the situations. Match the greeting form on the right with the situation on the left.

SITUATION   GREETING

a David is meeting a counterpart from the Dutch subsidiary at his office – they have only met once or twice before. What does David say?   *How was it?*

b A colleague of Jane Davis was transferred to Greece six months ago. She is back home for a couple of days. Jane greets her.   *How's it going?*

c A personal friend of David Hamilton has been in Mexico on business – they meet at a party.   *How are you?*

d A trainee is spending six months in Brussels gaining work experience. He spent some time, at the beginning of this period, in David Hamilton's office. They meet in the corridor.   *How are you enjoying life there?*

e David's secretary meets a good friend at a social function.

How are things?

f A colleague of Jane Davis is on a two-week sales course. She meets him by chance at the end of the first week.

How have you been getting on?

PRACTICE 3   Listen to the six dialogues from Practice 2 and note down the various replies to the enquiries. Complete the chart following the examples.

Enquiry	Positive reply	Negative reply	Actual reply
a *How are you?*	✓		Fine
b *How are you enjoying life there?*		✓	Not much
c *How was it?*			
d *How have you been getting on?*			
e *How are things?*			
f *How's it going?*			

Check your answers in the key.

PART 2   GREETING PEOPLE YOU SEE LESS FREQUENTLY

David Hamilton is at an international meeting in London for the various subsidiaries of ATI.

Comprehension Check   Listen to the three short dialogues in which David Hamilton greets various colleagues, and answer the questions.

1 Which of the dialogues took place

  a before a meeting?
  b at a social event?

2 When did David Hamilton last meet the three speakers

  a in Dialogue 4?
  b in Dialogue 5?
  c in Dialogue 6?

3 Identify the dialogues in which David is greeting someone he knows

  a just slightly.
  b well personally and at a business level.

Check your answers in the key.

Focus on Language   Listen to the dialogues again and complete the missing parts of the extracts, folowing the notes on the right. Then do the tasks that follow.

DIALOGUE 4   The style is **neutral**.

David	*Hello, Mr Inomata, _____. David Hamilton, we met at. . .*	NOTES David checks to see if Mr Inomata remembers him.
Mr Inomata	*Of course! _____, Mr Hamilton. You'd just moved over to Brussels when I was last there.. . .*	Greets him. This phrase suggests they have met before but only once.

Task   The three phrases below could also be used to greet people, but only one is appropriate in this situation.

It's great to see you.
I'm pleased to meet you again.
I'm pleased to see you.

DIALOGUE 5   The style is **neutral**.

Jacques	*Hello, David.*	NOTES
David	*Hello, Jacques. _____. I didn't _____.*	David shows he didn't expect this meeting.
Jacques	*Nor did I. Jean Grassi was due to come, but he couldn't manage it, so I'm here instead.*	
David	*I see. Well, _____, Jacques, it's been a long time. _____ in Paris?*	Greets him. Makes a general enquiry.
Jacques	*Pretty good. The autumn was a bit slow. . .And you, David. _____ Brussels?*	Redirects the conversation and makes a general enquiry.
David	*Yes. . .*	

> Check your answers in the key.

Task   Which of the three phrases below could be used to greet Jacques in this situation?

It's really great to see you.
It's nice to meet you again.
It's good to see you again.

DIALOGUE 6   The style is **informal.**

Sven   *Hi, David.*

David   *Sven. _____. You're looking well.*

Greets him and adds a compliment.

Sven   *Yes, I'm fine. A bit tired though. I just got back from the States yesterday.*

David   *Really. _____?*

Makes a general enquiry about the trip.

Sven   *The trip?*

David   *Yes. . .*

Task   Which of these sentences could David also use to enquire about Sven's trip?

Did you have a good time?
How was the trip?

Check your answers in the key.

Language Summary

Greetings

The following phrases can be used to greet people you only see from time to time. The phrases you choose will depend on how frequently you have met them before.

Greeting people you have met several times before	Greeting people you have met once before
NEUTRAL	**NEUTRAL**
It's very nice/good to see you again.	*I'm very pleased to meet you again.*
I'm (very) pleased to see you again.	*It's (very) nice to meet you again.*
INFORMAL	**INFORMAL**
Good/nice to see you.	*Good to meet you again.*
Great to see you.	*Pleased to meet you again.*

PRACTICE 4 Decide what you would say in the two situations below.
Follow the notes on the left which outline how the
conversation develops. The first part of each dialogue has
been done as an example.

SITUATION 1

You're meeting someone you know quite well at the
airport. You've just arrived, ten minutes late. The visitor is
already there waiting.

a Catch the person's attention.

Hello it's me.
John, I'm over here.
John. Hi, I've arrived.

b Greet the person. You haven't seen
each other for a while.

Good to see you again.
Good to meet you.
It's extremely nice to meet you again.

c Add a general enquiry.
The tone should be informal.

How's everything?
Are you well?
How are you getting on?

d Apologize for being late.

Have you been waiting long?
Unfortunately, my plane was late.
I'm sorry I've kept you waiting.

e Offer to help with the luggage.

Give me your bag please.
Let me give you a hand with your bags.
I want to help you with your bags.

SITUATION 2

While on a trip abroad you meet someone in the hotel. You
were introduced to this person at a conference a few years
ago, and have not met since. You are Philip Brooks.

a Greet the person.

Hello, Mr Ravelius.
Good morning, Mr Ravelius.
Hello, Peter.

b Check to see if the person remembers
you. Give your name.

I'm Mr Brooks. We met at. . .

*I don't know if you remember me. I'm
Philip Brooks. We met at. . .*

*Do you know me? Philip Brooks.
We met. . .*

c Greet the person. (Remember you've
only met this person once
before and then only briefly.)

I'm delighted to see you again.
It's nice to meet you again.
Good to see you again.

d Make an enquiry. (Make sure
it is not too informal.)

How have you been keeping?
How are things?
How are you?

PRACTICE 5 Complete the dialogue below between David Hamilton
and a colleague from Switzerland following the notes on the
right. Some phrases are suggested below. Keep the tone
friendly.

NOTES

Pierre *Hello, David.*

David *Hello, Pierre.* _____

Greet him. You
haven't seen him
for a while. Add a
general enquiry.

Pierre *Okay. We've been extremely busy and it looks as
if it's going to continue.* _____

Redirect the
conversation
back to David. You
have heard he has
been transferred to
the headquarters of
his company. Ask
about the job.

David *Okay, so far. Everything's going very smoothly and I'm
enjoying the challenge.*

Good to see you again.	*How's everything going?*
And yourself?	*Nice to see you again.*
How are you enjoying your new job?	*How's the new job going?*
What about you. . .?	*How are you?*
It's been a long time.	*I haven't seen you since last year.*

PRACTICE 6 Listen to the cassette. You will hear five instructions
asking you to greet various people. Stop the cassette after
each instruction and make your response. You will hear a
suggested answer after a pause.

Check your
answers in the key.

3

Concluding a conversation

Aims This unit shows how to bring a conversation to an end both with people you already know and with people who are more or less strangers.

PART 1 CONCLUDING A CONVERSATION WITH PEOPLE YOU KNOW

Background Emma Sanderson works for a small American industrial research organization in their European offices in Brussels.

Her work involves collecting data on the uses of various chemicals in different industries around Europe, and preparing reports for clients.

Comprehension Check Listen to the closing stages of three different conversations and answer the questions.

1 In which of the dialogues is Emma talking to

  a a colleague from her office?
  b her boss from the main office in the US?
  c a client?

2 Which of the conversations takes place

  a at the airport in Brussels just before someone takes a flight home?
  b in Emma's office towards the end of the meeting?
  c in the company restaurant after lunch?

3 In each of the dialogues when will the speakers see each other again?

4 In each of the dialogues which of the two speakers indicates it's time to end the conversation – Emma or the other person?

5 How well do you think Emma knows the other person in each of the dialogues?

  a Very well.
  b Well.
  c Just slightly.

> Check your answers in the key.

Focus on Language Listen to the dialogues again and complete the missing parts of the extracts, following the notes on the right. Then do the tasks that follow.

DIALOGUE 1 The style is **neutral**.

Mr Martinez *Yes, fine. _____, that seems to be everything so*

_____ and thank you. It's been a very useful meeting.

Emma *Good. Well, goodbye Mr Martinez,*
I'll _____ in a couple of months.

NOTES

Indicates that he wants to end the conversation.

Says goodbye and also thanks her.

Says goodbye and at the same time refers to their next meeting.

Task The next meeting will be in a couple of months. Does this mean that *it will be in two months exactly* or *about two months?*

DIALOGUE 2 The style is **informal.**

Emma *I _____ be going. I've got a client coming in at three and I want to look through his file.*

NOTES

Indicates that she wants to end the conversation.

Tom *Okay. _____ then. _____ goes well.*

Says goodbye and at the same time wishes her a successful meeting.

Emma *Thanks Tom, _____*

Says goodbye.

Task Emma indicated she wanted to end the conversation by saying *I really must be going.* Which of the following three phrases could also be used in this situation?

Right, it's time to go.
Would you mind if I leave?
I'm afraid I've got to go.

DIALOGUE 3 The style is **informal.**

Brad *Anyway, Emma, they're calling my flight so _____ get going. I don't want to have to rush like last time.*

NOTES

Indicates he wants to end the conversation.

Emma *Okay Brad, goodbye and _____ back.*

Says goodbye and at the same time wishes him a pleasant flight.

Brad *Sure thing. I'll _____ in the fall and we can go through ...*

Refers to their next meeting. Note: The fall is an American expression for the autumn.

Task The two phrases below could also be used when saying goodbye to people at an airport. Choose the one that Emma could also have used in this context.

Goodbye Brad, I do hope you have a most enjoyable flight back.
I'll say goodbye. Enjoy the flight.

Check your answers in the key.

**Language
Summary**

Ending a conversation

The way a conversation is concluded varies according to
the situation.

If you know when you'll see the other person again, it's
usual to refer to this next meeting, e.g.

Goodbye, I'll see you next week.

If you know something about the other person's
immediate plans, you can refer to these, e.g.

Goodbye and have a good holiday.

If you have received help or hospitality add your thanks
when you say goodbye, e.g.

Goodbye and thank you very much for all your help.

Saying goodbye	Comment
NEUTRAL Goodbye.	*I'll look forward to seeing you when you're next in London/next time you're here.* *I'll see you in a couple of months/on Monday.* *I'll see you later (the same day).* *(I hope you) enjoy the rest of your trip.* *(I hope you) have a good flight back.* *I hope the meeting goes well.* *Thank you very much for the meal.* *Thank you for all your help/everything.*
INFORMAL Bye. Bye. See you later	*See you soon/in a few days/sometime next week.* *(and) enjoy the film.* *(and) have a good weekend.* *(and) thanks for everything.*

PRACTICE 1   Conclude conversations in the six situations below.
Choose phrases similar to those in the list above.

EXAMPLE
Somebody who works in your department is about to
leave on a week's business trip to Japan.

_Goodbye_____ Marcello, I _hope the trip_____

_goes_____

a You are about to leave your office for the evening. One
of the people you work with is still there.

_____, Isabel. _____
evening.

b You are seeing an important customer off at the airport.
This visitor comes over to see you at least once a month.

_Goodbye, Alain. I'll_____
sometime next month._

c You have been visiting the production facilities at your
Swiss subsidiary. Your contact there obviously put a lot
of effort into organizing this visit.

_Goodbye, Mr Heinig and_____
everything._

d You are saying goodbye to a visitor outside his hotel.
He is flying back to Ireland tomorrow evening.

_Goodbye, Shaun. I_____ a good
flight back tomorrow._

e Your department has just been visited by the financial
controller from your headquarters in Holland. He visits
you from time to time.

_Goodbye, Mr King and we'll_____
seeing you when_____ next over
here._

PRACTICE 2   Look at the information in the chart on the next page and
then decide how you would say goodbye to each person.
The first one has been done as an example.

EXAMPLE
_Goodbye, Margaret. Have a good holiday and I'll see you
when you get back._

Person	Situation	Next probable meeting
Margaret Daniels. Same department as you.	She is about to leave for a two-week holiday.	When she gets back.
a Anna Marcos Secretary at company you are visiting.	You are at the end of a month's visit. She was responsible for all the arrangements for you.	
b John Dennis. Your American counterpart.	He is spending two days in your department and is about to leave at the end of the first day.	Tomorrow 9 a.m.
c Jan Kruger. A frequent visitor to your company from Denmark.	He is about to leave for his return flight home.	In Denmark. Meeting with him next month, date not fixed.

PRACTICE 3   Read the situation and then complete the dialogue
following the notes on the right.

SITUATION

Ramon Gomez is on a two-year assignment to his
European headquarters in London. He is about to leave for
a month's holiday and is speaking to a colleague of his.

NOTES

Colleague   *When are you leaving Ramon?*

Ramon   *In about half an hour. I want to get away before
the traffic gets bad.*

Colleague   *Okay. Well, _____ now and
_____ holiday.*

Says goodbye and
wishes him a
pleasant holiday.

Ramon   *I'm sure I will. I'm really looking forward to a month of
good food and sun.*

Colleague   *I bet. Anyway, _____ and
_____ when you get back.*

Repeats his
wishes and refers
to the next meeting.

> Check your answers in the key.

Language Summary

Indicating you want to end a conversation

In some situations it may be necessary to indicate to a person when you want to conclude a conversation. For example if you were having lunch with somebody and you were worried that you would be late for another appointment.

Phrases indicating you want to end the conversation	Explanation
I really must be going.	*They are calling my flight.*
I really must be leaving.	*It's rather late and I've got an early morning meeting.*
I really should be getting back to my hotel.	*It's getting very late and I've got an early morning flight.*
I think I really should be going.	*I've got a lot to do this afternoon.*

PRACTICE 4

What would you say in the following situations to indicate that you want to end the conversation? Read the situations on the left and then match them with an appropriate phrase on the right.

SITUATION

a You have been invited out to dinner while on business. It's now 12.30 a.m. and you are feeling very tired.

b You have been discussing a contract with a British supplier. You feel the relevant points have been discussed.

c A colleague has driven you to the station and is standing talking to you. You're worried you will miss the train.

d You're having lunch with a friend. It's now 2 p.m. You have an appointment at 2.30.

e You have had lunch at a colleague's home and you are now ready to leave.

PHRASE

I really must go, Tom, or I'll miss my train.

I really should be going, David. I've got an appointment at 2.30.

I think I should be getting back to the hotel. It's getting rather late.

I think that's everything, Mr Fish. We've covered all the points we need to discuss for the moment.

It's been a very nice afternoon, but I think I should be leaving. I've got some things to prepare for tomorrow's meeting.

PRACTICE 5   How would you indicate you want to end a conversation in the following situations?

a You have been for a drink with some of the other participants on the same computer course as you. It's now late and you have to prepare something for tomorrow.

b You are being seen off at the airport. Your flight has been called but the other person keeps on talking.

c You are having lunch with a group of friends. It's now 2.30 p.m. and you know you have a lot of work to do at the office.

d You have spent a very nice evening with an English family you met while on business. It's now 11.30 p.m. and you feel you should leave.

Check your answers in the key.

PART 2   CONCLUDING A CONVERSATION WITH PEOPLE YOU DON'T KNOW

Background   Emma Sanderson is on business in Germany. She has arranged interviews in various companies in Frankfurt and Munich. The object is to collect data on chemicals for insulation materials.

Comprehension Check   Listen to the closing stages of two different dialogues and answer the questions.

1 Which of the two conversations does not take place in an office?

2 Who do you think she's talking to in each extract?

3 In which of the dialogues has Emma met the other person

a by prior arrangement?

b by chance?

Check your answers in the key.

Focus on Language   Listen to the dialogues again and complete the missing parts of the extracts, following the notes on the right.

DIALOGUE 4   The style is **neutral**.

Emma   *Well, goodbye Dr Lenk. It's _____ you. Thank you very much for giving up so much of your time.*

NOTES

Says goodbye and makes a positive comment about the meeting.

Dr Lenk   *That's all right. . .*

DIALOGUE 5 The style is **neutral**.

Passenger   *Right, here you are. Have you got it?*

Emma   *Yes, thanks. So goodbye. I've _____ you.*

Passenger   *Goodbye, and don't . . .*

> Check your answers in the key.

Language Summary

Ending conversations with people you do not know

When concluding a conversation with people you have only just met and probably will not meet again, the following phrases can be used.

Goodbye.	*I have enjoyed meeting you.* *It's been nice meeting you.* *I have enjoyed talking to you.* *It's been interesting talking to you.*

PRACTICE 6 How would you conclude conversations in the three situations below? Use the verbs in brackets following the example.

EXAMPLE
You are travelling by plane to Frankfurt. The plane has just landed. Say goodbye to the person sitting next to you.

Goodbye. I have enjoyed talking (talk) to you.

a You have spent an evening with a colleague and his wife. Say goodbye to another guest.

Goodbye. I _____ (meet) you.

b You have been eating alone in a restaurant in London. Say goodbye to the people sitting at the next table who you spoke to a lot during the meal.

I'll be going now. It _____ (talk) you.

c You have been visiting an American company. Say goodbye to another visitor who you were introduced to.

Goodbye, Mr Phillips.
It _____ (meet) you.

PRACTICE 7 Listen to the cassette. You will be given instructions to conclude different conversations. You will hear a suggested answer after a pause.

> Check your answers in the key.

4

Inviting

Aims   This unit shows you how to
- invite people
- accept or decline invitations

PART 1 INVITING AND ACCEPTING

Background

Brian Duke works for a British computer firm. His work frequently involves entertaining, particularly overseas clients.

Comprehension Check

Listen to three short conversations Brian Duke had with different people and answer the questions.

1 In which dialogue is Brian Duke inviting
   a a colleague in his company?
   b a business associate, visiting his company?

2 What kind of invitation does Brian make in each case?

3 Are the invitations accepted or declined?

4 In which of the dialogues does Brian know the person he is inviting
   a very well?
   b quite well?

> Check your answers in the key.

Focus on Language

Listen to the dialogues again and complete the missing parts of the extracts, following the notes on the right. Then do the tasks that follow.

DIALOGUE 1 The style is **neutral**.

NOTES

Brian *Well, er, my wife and I have invited some friends for dinner tomorrow and, if you haven't any plans,*

_____ ?

Leads into the invitation.

Makes the invitation. The form shows that he is unsure if she will accept the invitation.

Christina _____ Brian. I'd _____

Thanks and accepts.

Task Which of the sentences below could also be used to accept the invitation in this situation?

Thanks. What time should I come?
That's very nice of you. I'll look forward to it.

DIALOGUE 2 The style is **neutral**.

NOTES

Brian *Well, if you like English cooking, _____ ?*
Maybe sometime next week before you go back to Sweden.

Leads into the invitation. Makes the invitation.

Lars *Yes, that _____ , Brian.*
I'd _____

Thanks and accepts.

Tasks Which of the sentences below could also be used to:

a make Brian's invitation?

Perhaps you'd like to have dinner at my house.
We wanted to invite you for dinner.

b accept this invitation?

Yes, that sounds great, thanks.
Oh, thank you very much. I'll look forward to that.

DIALOGUE 3 The style is **informal.**

Brian *Not bad for one day. Oh, John, some of us are going for a drink after the exhibition has finished.*
_____?

John *Thanks. _____. Where shall we meet?*

NOTES

Leads into the invitation.

Makes the invitation.

Accepts.

Tasks Which of the sentences below could also be used to:

a make Brian's invitation?

I was wondering if you'd like to join us.
Why don't you come?

b accept this invitation?

Yes, that sounds good, thanks.
Yes, thank you very much indeed, Brian.
It would be a pleasure.

Check your
answers in the key.

Language Summary **Inviting**

Invitations can be made in a *neutral* or *informal* way, depending on how well the people know each other.

On first contact or when people know each other only slightly and at a business level use a neutral invitation. This is the most usual type of invitation. At a more personal level where people know each other very well, use informal invitations.

NEUTRAL INVITATIONS

I was wondering if you would like to join us for a meal.
Would you like to visit a typical German Weinstube?

INFORMAL INVITATIONS

How about going to a musical tonight?
Why don't you join us for a drink?
What about going out for a meal?
Why not come round for a drink?

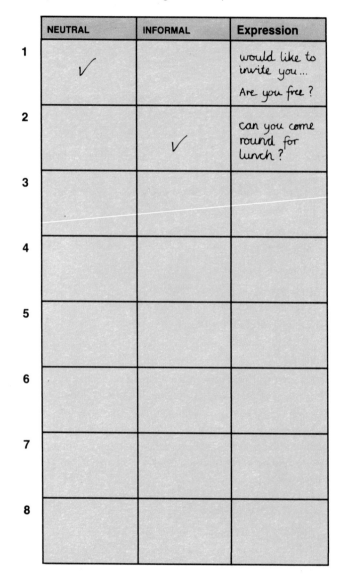

PRACTICE 1 Listen to the cassette. You will hear eight invitations. Say if the style of the invitations is *neutral* or *informal,* and write down the expressions used.

Complete the chart following the examples.

	NEUTRAL	INFORMAL	Expression
1	✓		would like to invite you... Are you free?
2		✓	can you come round for lunch?
3			
4			
5			
6			
7			
8			

PRACTICE 2 Make an appropriate invitation for the following four situations.

a You have been showing a foreign visitor around your department. You have some tickets for the theatre for tomorrow evening and want to invite him. You have met him several times before and know that he likes theatre.

b You have just finished a meeting with a potential customer. You want to invite him out for a meal tonight. This is the first contact.

c You want to invite an American neighbour and his wife for a drink at the weekend. You know them quite well.

d You are attending a residential seminar. There are tennis facilities near by and you have arranged to play. Invite one of the other participants. You have got to know this person quite well during this week.

> Check your answers in the key.

Language Summary

Accepting invitations

When accepting invitations it is usual to combine a phrase of thanks with a phrase accepting the invitation. The following phrases can all be combined to accept invitations.

Thanking	Accepting
NEUTRAL	
Thank you very much.	*That would be very nice.*
That's very kind of you.	*I'd like that very much.*
Thank you for inviting me.	*I'd love to come.*
	I'd be delighted to come.
	I'll look forward to it.
INFORMAL	
Thanks.	*That's a good idea.*
	What a good idea.
	That sounds fun.

PRACTICE 3

Choose the most appropriate combination from the sentences above to reply to the invitations.

EXAMPLE

If you're free tomorrow evening, would you like to go to the theatre? I've got a spare ticket.

Thank you <u>very much</u> .
That would <u>be very nice</u> .
I'll <u>look forward to it</u>

a *Mario, what about a game of tennis this evening?*

   Yes, Tom, _____ .
   That's _____ .

b *Mr Jones, I was wondering if you would be free to have dinner this evening.*

   Yes, that's _____ .
   I'd like _____ .

c *Would you like to come over for a drink at the weekend?*
Both you and your wife.

Yes, we'd like _____ .
That's _____ .

PRACTICE 4   Reorganize the sentences below into two separate dialogues. In each dialogue Brian Duke is one of the speakers. He is inviting a visitor out for a meal.

Dialogue A

1 *That's very kind of you. I'd like that very much.*

2 *If you've nothing arranged this evening, Mr Vane, I was wondering if you'd like to come out for a meal with us.*

3 *Fine. I'll look forward to it.*

4 *Good. I'll pick you up at the hotel, about eight then.*

Dialogue B

1 *Fine. About what time?*

2 *Good. Shall I pick you up at the hotel?*

3 *I don't know what your plans are, Paul, but would you like to go out for a meal on Thursday evening?*

4 *Thanks very much. I'd love to.*

5 *Shall we say half past seven?*

> Check your answers in the key.

PART 2 INVITING AND DECLINING

Sometimes it is not possible to accept an invitation. You have to decline.

Comprehension Check   Listen to Brian Duke inviting another customer, Jules Ferrier, to have dinner with him and answer the questions below.

1 What kind of invitation is it?
2 Jules cannot accept the invitation. What reason does he give?

> Check your answers in the key.

Focus on Language   Listen to the dialogue again and complete the missing parts of the extract, following the notes on the right.

DIALOGUE 4   The style is **neutral**.

NOTES

Brian   *Oh, then, if you're free this evening perhaps you'd like to come round for a meal. Nothing special but ...*

Makes the invitation.

Jules   *That's* _____ *, Brian,*
_____ *I can.*
It's my last night and ...

Thanks but declines.

> Check your answers in the key.

Language Summary

Declining invitations

When declining an invitation it is usual to thank the person for the invitation, then decline and finally give a reason. The following phrases can all be combined to decline invitations.

Thanking	Declining	Reason
NEUTRAL		
Thank you for inviting me	*but I'm afraid I can't come.*	*I've already arranged something else.*
Thank you very much,	*but unfortunately*	*I won't be here tomorrow.*
That's very kind of you	*but I can't.*	*I'm busy on Thursday.*
INFORMAL		
Thanks	*but I can't make it then.*	*I play squash every Monday.*

PRACTICE 5   Listen to five short invitations. In each case the invitation is declined.

As you listen, pick out the expression used to decline the invitation and complete the chart below.

	Actual words used	Explanation
1		
2		
3		
4		
5		

PRACTICE 6   While Brian Duke was on business in Sweden he was invited out to eat on two separate occasions, first by someone he knew very well, and then by a new contact.

The two incomplete dialogues below refer to these two invitations. Complete them by following the notes on the right.

DIALOGUE A   The style is **informal**.

Sven   *Brian, look if* _____,

why don't we _____?

Brian   _____, *Sven,* _____
I'm already having dinner with Arne Brandsberg.
_____ *tomorrow night?*

Sven   *Yes, that's fine for me. What time?*

NOTES

Leads into the invitation by checking to see if Brian has any plans. Invites him out for a meal.

Thanks but declines.

Suggests an alternative date.

DIALOGUE B   The style is **neutral**.

Jan   *Do you know Malmö at all, Brian?*

Brian   *No, this is my first visit.*

Jan   *Well, if* _____ *tonight,*
I was _____ *if* _____
this evening. Then I can show you something of the town.

Brian   *That's* _____
I'm _____

NOTES

Leads into the invitation by checking to see if Brian is busy. Makes an invitation to look round the town.

Thanks him for the invitation but declines. He has other plans.

PRACTICE 7   Listen to the cassette. You will hear five instructions asking you to respond to various invitations. Make your response after each instruction.

Check your answers in the key.

5

Thanking and showing appreciation

Aims This unit shows you how to

- thank people for their hospitality
- thank people for helping you
- respond when people thank you for hospitality or help

PART 1   THANKING PEOPLE FOR HOSPITALITY

Background

Philippe Blanchard works for the French subsidiary of an American multi-national. On visits abroad he is often entertained and must thank people for their hospitality.

Comprehension Check

Listen to three short dialogues in which Philippe Blanchard is thanking various people for their hospitality.

1 Where do you think the three dialogues take place?

2 What kind of hospitality has Philippe received in each case?

3 In which dialogue has he only met the other person recently?

> Check your answers in the key.

Focus on Language

Listen to the dialogues again and complete the missing parts of the extracts, following the notes on the right. Then do the tasks that follow.

DIALOGUE 1   The style is **informal**.

Philippe   *So should I. Well, _____ lunch, Frank. _____.*

NOTES

Thanks his host.
Adds a positive comment.

Frank   *Good, _____ it. Next time ...*

Responds to Philippe's thanks.

Tasks   Which of the two sentences could also be used to thank people in this situation?

a *It was most kind of you to invite me for lunch; it was quite delicious.*
It was a good lunch; thanks for inviting me.

b What other phrase could be used to make Philippe's positive comment about the meal? Make a sentence using *I/enjoy/meal/very much.*

DIALOGUE 2   The style is **neutral**.

Philippe   *Anyway, _____ organizing the evening, David.*

NOTES

Thanks his host.
Adds a positive comment.

David   *_____, Philippe. It's had mixed reviews but ...*

Responds to Philippe's thanks.

Task   The two responses below could also be used to thank people for this type of invitation but only one is appropriate in this situation.

It was very kind of you to organize the evening. It was a really good play.
I would like to thank you very much for organizing the evening. It was an excellent play.

DIALOGUE 3   The style is **neutral.**

Philippe   *Yes, it's _____.*

NOTES

Makes a positive comment.

It _____. I hope it hasn't been too much trouble.

Thanks his hostess.

Hostess   *Not at all. _____. I hope you'll come and stay ...*

Responds to his thanks.

Tasks   **a** Philippe described the weekend in a very positive way. Which of these descriptive words below could also be used?

Nice/enjoyable/good/wonderful

b The two responses below can also be used to thank people, but only one is appropriate in this situation.

Thanks for everything. It's been fun.
Thank you very much for all your hospitality. I really appreciate it.

> Check your
> answers in the key.

Language Summary   **Thanking people for hospitality**

When thanking people for hospitality, it is usual to combine a *phrase of thanks* with a *positive comment* to show your appreciation.

Phrase of thanks	Positive comment
NEUTRAL	
Thank you very much. I really appreciate your hospitality.	*It's been a very pleasant weekend.*
It was very kind of you to invite me.	*You really have a lovely house.*
Thank you very much for the meal.	*It's an excellent restaurant.*
Thank you very much for organizing this evening.	*The meal was delicious.*
Thank you very much for everything.	*I have enjoyed myself.*
INFORMAL	
Thanks for asking me out.	*It was great fun.*
Thanks for the meal.	*It was very good.*
Thanks Tom.	*I enjoyed that.*

PRACTICE 1   Read the six situations below and then choose one of the
phrases on the right to thank your host.

SITUATION	PHRASE OF THANKS
a A friend has bought you coffee.	*Thank you for all your hospitality. I really have appreciated it.*
b You have been taken out to the theatre to see a comedy by the Marketing Director of a company you do business with.	*Thank you for getting me a ticket.*
c You have just spent two months in another of your company's subsidiaries. The people there have been very friendly and invited you out a lot.	*Thank you very much for the meal.*
d While in London some friends of yours took you to see the Wimbledon final.	*It was most kind of you to invite me over.*
e A potential supplier you have been visiting took you out for dinner.	*Thanks, David.*
f While on a business trip your counterpart invited you to spend a day at his home.	*It was very nice of you to invite me. I really enjoyed the play.*

PRACTICE 2   Now go back to the situations in Practice 1 and decide how
you would complete the thanks by adding an appropriate
comment from the list below.

EXAMPLE

SITUATION a   *I needed that.*

It's been a useful two months.   *I've enjoyed myself a lot.*
It was very funny.   *It was delicious.*
It was a very exciting match.

PRACTICE 3   Following the conversation notes on the left, decide how
to thank your host in the following situations.

SITUATION 1

A business contact of yours organized a trip to the theatre
for you.

a Thank your host (you don't know   *It was very kind of*
this person very well).   *you to invite me.*

b Tell him or her you enjoyed the play.   _____

c Compliment him or her on the choice.   _____

SITUATION 2

You are staying with some English friends for a weekend.
You met them on holiday last year.

a Thank them for inviting you.   _____

b Compliment them on the place.   _____

c Tell them how much you have   _____
enjoyed the weekend.

SITUATION 3

You have been on business overseas. A potential customer
has invited you for a meal in a very good restaurant.

a Compliment him or her on the meal.   _____

b Thank him or her for inviting you.   _____
(Remember it's a first contact.)

c Tell him or her how much you like the   _____
restaurant.

> Check your
> answers in the key.

PART 2 RESPONDING TO THANKS

Background
Philippe Blanchard is now attending a week's
management training course in the company's European
headquarters in London.

Comprehension Check
Listen to three short dialogues in which you will hear him
thanking various people who have helped him in some way.
Then answer the questions below.

1 What help has he received in each dialogue?

2 In which dialogue is he speaking to:

  a someone working at the training centre?
  b a receptionist at the hotel?
  c someone on the staff at headquarters?

3 Say in which of the situations the person Philippe is
thanking has made *special* efforts for him?

> Check your
> answers in the key.

Focus on Language
Listen to the dialogues again and complete the missing
parts of the extracts, following the notes on the right.

		NOTES
DIALOGUE 4	The style is **neutral**.	
Philippe	*They look very good, Mike. _____.*	Thanks him for his
	I hope it didn't take you too long.	help.
Mike	*No, really _____. I did it one afternoon*	Responds to his
	when ...	thanks.

		NOTES
DIALOGUE 5	The style is **neutral**.	
Man	*If you go up to the fifth floor, they'll be able to help you.*	
Philippe	*Thank you very much.*	Thanks him.
Man	*You're _____.*	Responds to his
		thanks.

		NOTES
DIALOGUE 6	The style is **neutral**.	
Receptionist	*There's a message for you, Mr Blanchard. Here you are.*	
Philippe	*Thank you very much.*	Thanks her.
Receptionist	*_____ it.*	Responds to his
		thanks.

> Check your answers in the key.

Language Summary

Responding to thanks

When a person is being thanked for giving help, the
following phrases can be used to respond.

Thanking phrase	Response
Thanking people for personal help	
Thank you for all your help.	*That's quite all right.*
Thank you very much for finding	*That's okay.*
out about the theatre.	*It was no trouble.*
Thanking people for a service	
Thanks for the information.	*You're welcome.*
Thank you.	*Don't mention it.*
Thank you very much.	*That's okay/all right.*

PRACTICE 4   In the following incomplete dialogues Philippe is thanking
people for different kinds of help. Decide how to respond
to his thanks in each situation. Complete the dialogues
following the example.

SITUATION
Philippe is thanking another participant on the course for
a lift back to his hotel.

EXAMPLE

Philippe   *See you tomorrow Angela and thanks for the lift. I hope it hasn't taken you out of your way.*

Angela   *That's _____ all right _____ Philippe, I live quite near here anyway.*

SITUATION 1

Phillipe is thanking an airline clerk for flight information to the States for his summer holiday.

Philippe   *Thank you for the information.*

Airline Clerk   *You're _____ .*

SITUATION 2

Philippe is thanking the Course Organizer's secretary for some typing and photocopying she did for him during the course.

Philippe   *Goodbye, and thank you for all your help. I hope it hasn't made a lot of extra work for you.*

Secretary   *That's _____ Mr Blanchard. Really, it was _____ .*

SITUATION 3

Philippe is about to leave the course. He is thanking the Organizer Derek Thompson.

Philippe   *Thanks for everything Derek. It's been a very useful two weeks.*

Organizer   *Good, I'm _____ it.*

SITUATION 4

Philippe is thanking an airport official at Heathrow. He has just directed him to the check-in.

Airline Official   *If you go down these stairs you will see the check-in desk to your left.*

Philippe   *Thank you very much.*

Airline Official   *Don't _____ it.*

PRACTICE 5   You will hear extracts from six short conversations in which people are thanking others for hospitality or general help. After you listen to each one, stop the cassette and respond. You will hear a suggested answer after a pause.

Check your answers in the key.

Offering and requesting

Aims   This unit shows you how to

- offer help to people in various ways
- respond when people offer help or hospitality
- ask people for their help

PART 1 OFFERING

Background   Helga Müller has recently arrived in the UK to spend a month in the British subsidiary of her company. The objective of this visit is to see the new computer system in operation. She is staying with the Marketing Manager Bill Seeley who she has known for many years.

Comprehension Check   Listen to three short dialogues and answer the questions.

1 Which of the dialogues takes place

 a at a party?
 b at Bill's home?
 c at one of the sales branches?

2 What exactly is being offered in each dialogue?

3 Are the offers of help accepted or declined in each dialogue?

> Check your
> answers in the key.

Focus on Language   Listen to the dialogues again and complete the missing parts of the extracts, following the notes on the right. Then do the tasks that follow.

DIALOGUE 1   The style is **informal**.

Bill   *Hiring a car is terribly expensive.*
_____ borrow our second car? It's a VW and I expect you're used to driving one of those.

NOTES
Makes his offer.

Helga   *_____, Bill. Are you sure you don't need it?*

Accepts his offer.

Task   Which of the two sentences below could also be used to make Bill's offer of his car.

How about borrowing our second car?
We would be very pleased if you would borrow our second car.

DIALOGUE 2   The style is **neutral**.

Mr Jeffrey   *I'm glad you found the visit useful, Mrs Müller. By the way, how are you getting back to town? _____ a taxi?*

NOTES
Makes his offer.

Helga   *Thank you, but _____. Mr Seeley has lent me a car ...*

Declines his offer.

Task   Which of the two sentences below could also be used to say no to the offer?

That's very kind of you but no thank you.
No thanks.

DIALOGUE 3 The style is **neutral**.

NOTES

Helga   *Well, I haven't got any children of school age, but my neighbours may be interested. _____ to give you their address?*

Makes her offer.

Woman   *Yes please, I'd _____*

Accepts her offer.

Task   Which of the two phrases below could also be used to offer the address?

Do you want their address?
If you like, I could give you their address.

Check your
answers in the key.

Language Summary

Offering help and hospitality

The following phrases can be used to offer hospitality and help. Notice that nearly all offers are made by asking a question.

NEUTRAL

Would you like a cup of coffee?
Would you like a lift back to your hotel?
Shall I pick you up at the airport?
Would you like me to try to change the tickets?

INFORMAL

How about going for a cup of coffee?
Do you want another cup of coffee?
Do you want me to photocopy this for you?

PRACTICE 1   Read the six situations and then choose one of the offers of help on the right for each situation. Follow the example.

SITUATION

OFFER

a You are meeting someone at the airport. He arrives with two heavy cases.

Can I get you all another drink?

b You have been out for a meal with some friends. One of them lives near you. He hasn't got a car.

Would you like me to book you a room in the local hotel?

c At an exhibition someone expresses interest in your products

Let me give you a hand with your bags.

d You are having a drink with some of the other participants on a computer course you are attending.

If you like, I could put some brochures in the post.

e You are phoning a customer about arrangements for his visit.

Do you want a lift?

PRACTICE 2 A visitor has just arrived in your company. He has a meeting with one of your colleagues who is going to be a little late. You have been asked to look after this visitor. What would you say in the following situations?

EXAMPLE
Offer him a seat while he waits.

Would _you like to take_ a seat until Mrs Valmin arrives?

a Offer to take his coat.

Let me _____

b Offer him some refreshment, coffee, etc.

Shall I _____?

c Offer to show him some company literature.

Would you _____?

d Offer to organize a trip round the factory for him.

If _____,
I would _____.

e Offer your general help.

Let me know if there's anything else
_____

> Check your
> answers in the key.

Language Summary

Accepting and declining offers	
Offering	**Accepting**
Would you like me to get you some tickets for the theatre?	*Yes please.* *Yes, if you're sure it's no trouble.* *Yes, that's very kind of you.* *Yes, that would be very nice.*
Offering	**Declining**
Would you like a cup of coffee? *Would you like me to call you a taxi?*	*No thank you.* *Thank you, but no.* *Thank you but it's not necessary. I can easily walk.* *Thank you but really don't bother. It's quite near and I'd enjoy the walk.*

PRACTICE 3 Listen to four short dialogues in which various people respond to offers of help. What are the offers? Say whether they are accepted or declined. Write down the expressions used. Follow the example.

Offer	Accepted	Declined	Expression used
a book a room in a hotel		✓	No thanks… It's really not necessary.
b			
c			
d			

PRACTICE 4 Complete the short two-line dialogues below according to the instructions in **bold**.

EXAMPLE

Speaker 1 *David, can I get you another coffee?*

Speaker 2 **Decline** No, thank you. Not at the moment.

a Speaker 1 *I know you're very busy tomorrow so if you like I could show Mr Orsini round the factory.*

Speaker 2 **Decline** (You have already asked another colleague to do it.)

b Speaker 1 *Do you want me to pick Mr Davis up at his hotel? It's not far from where I live.*

Speaker 2 **Decline** (You plan to order him a taxi.)

c Speaker 1 *There's an excellent play on at the theatre. Shall I get some tickets for tomorrow?*

Speaker 2 **Decline** (You are going out.)

> Check your answers in the key.

PART 2   MAKING REQUESTS

Background   Helga Müller is on her way to visit another sales branch.

Comprehension Check   Listen to two short dialogues which take place on her way to the branch and answer the questions.

1 Where is she, and what has happened?

2 What kind of help is she asking for?

3 Why can't the person in the first dialogue help?

> Check your answers in the key.

Focus on Language   Listen to the dialogues again and complete the missing parts of the extracts, following the notes on the right.

DIALOGUE 4   The style is **neutral**.

Helga   *Excuse me, _____? My car's broken down and I need to push it off the road.*

NOTES

Asks for help.

Passer-by   *_____, I'm already late for a dental appointment ...*

Refuses to help, explaining why it's not possible.

DIALOGUE 5   The style is **neutral**.

Helga   *Excuse me, _____ to push my car off the road? It's just broken down.*

NOTES

Asks for help.

Passer-by   *_____. Where do you want it to go? ...*

Agrees to help ...

> Check your answers in the key.

Language Summary   **Making requests**

The following phrases can be used to ask for things and for different kinds of help.

> *Can I have a cup of coffee?*
> *Could you pour me some more wine?*
> *Could you possibly pick me up at the station?*
> *Do you think you could type this up for me?*
> *Would it be possible for you to make a short speech before dinner?*

PRACTICE 5   The chart below summarizes six situations where you want different types of help. Decide on the best way of making your request in each situation.

Person	Situation	Request
Waiter	You have just finished a meal.	Bill
a Customer	You arranged an appointment for next Tuesday, now it's not possible.	Change the date
b Secretary in company you are visiting	The meeting is over. You want to return to your hotel.	A taxi
c Your host	You have been invited for the weekend by your counterpart.	To ring home
d A colleague	You arranged to show a visitor round the department. You are very busy.	Show visitor round instead of you
e Passer-by	You need coins for a pay phone.	Change for £1

EXAMPLE

Can ___*I have*___ the bill, please?

a Would _____ change the date of
our meeting?

b Could you _____ a taxi?

c Do you think _____ home?

d David, would _____
Mr Weiss _____ the department?

> Check your
> answers in the key.

e Can _____ change for £1?

Language Summary   **Responding to requests**

The following phrases can be used to respond to requests.

Request	Replies	
	Positive	**Negative**
Could you get me some tickets for the concert tomorrow?	*Certainly.* *Of course.* *Yes, that's no problem.*	*I'm afraid not. It's fully booked.* *I'm sorry that isn't possible. There aren't any seats left.* *I'm sorry but I don't think there are any tickets left.*

PRACTICE 6 Listen to five more requests and say if the replies are positive or negative. Write down the expressions used. Complete the chart below following the example.

Request	Reply		Expression used
	Negative	**Positive**	
a look at Someone's paper		✓	Yes, of course.
b			
c			
d			
e			

PRACTICE 7 Complete the dialogues below, following the instructions in **bold.** Follow the example.

EXAMPLE

Speaker 1 *I'm thinking of going to the theatre while I'm here. Could you ring up and find out what's on.*

Speaker 2 **Affirmative** Certanly. I'll give them a ring as soon as I've finished this.

a Speaker 1 *Excuse me. My watch has stopped. Can you tell me the time?*

Speaker 2 **Negative** (Say you are not wearing a watch.)

b Speaker 1 *John, do you think you could give a short welcoming speech before the meeting?*

Speaker 2 **Affirmative**

c Speaker 1 *Do you think we could possibly meet an hour earlier?*

Speaker 2 **Negative** (Say you have another meeting.)

d Speaker 1 *Could you have a quick look at this report before tomorrow morning?*

Speaker 2 **Negative** *(Say you are terribly busy.)*

Check your answers in the key.

7

The first
five minutes

Aims   This unit revises much of the language used in Units 1–6, in particular, greetings and introductions. In addition, it also shows you how to

- start up conversations with people you do not know very well
- keep conversations moving by asking general questions

PART 1 CONVERSATIONS WHEN MEETING PEOPLE

Background Richard Dyson works in the sales department of Celito, a British company producing industrial adhesive tape. He is planning a sales trip to Germany.

Predicting the Conversation Read the two telexes below which refer to Richard Dyson's trip to Germany.

Then decide what the two men will talk about in the first few minutes of their conversation when they meet at the airport.

```
ATTENTION GERHARD WEISS

RE YOUR TELEPHONE CALL YESTERDAY 17 JAN. WE HAVE
NOW FINALISED ARRANGEMENTS FOR RICHARD DYSON'S
TRAVEL ON MON 12 FEB. HE WILL ARRIVE DUSSELDORF AIRPORT
FLIGHT BA 786 16.40. PLEASE BOOK HOTEL
ACCOMMODATION CENTRAL DUSSELDORF.

PLEASE INFORM US BY RETURN WHO HE SHOULD CONTACT
AND WHERE.

REGARDS.

MELANIE HUGHES PA EXPORT SALES MANAGER CELITO
UK
```

```
ATTENTION MELANIE HUGHES

WE CONFIRM MR DYSON WILL BE MET BY MR WEISS MON
12 FEB, DUSSELDORF AIRPORT. 16.40. ROOM BOOKED AT
THE PLAZA HOTEL.

PLEASE ASK MR DYSON TO BRING SAMPLES OF NOS 3566,
8976. 456. 901 AS WE ARE MOST INTERESTED.

GERHARD WEISS PURCHASING DEPARTMENT
```

Check your answers in the key.

Comprehension Check

Listen to the first part of Dialogue 1 which takes place on Richard Dyson's arrival at the airport. He is being met by Gerhard Weiss and his assistant.

Say if the following statements are **true** or **false**.

1 Richard Dyson has met both men before.
2 Dieter Brand works in the same department as Weiss as his assistant.
3 The flight was very good.
4 Richard Dyson travelled on Lufthansa.
5 Richard Dyson brought all the samples with him.

Check your answers in the key.

Focus on Language

Now listen to the extract again and answer the questions.

1 Gerhard opens the conversation by greeting Richard. What does he say?
2 Richard thanks Gerhard for meeting him. What does he say?
3 He then introduces his colleague Dieter Brand.
Richard, _____ my assistant, Dieter Brand.
4 Richard apologizes for not bringing one of the samples. What does he say and what reason does he give?
5 Richard thanks Gerhard again for meeting him. What does he say?

Check your answers in the key.

Language Summary

Conversation starters

Often the first few minutes of a conversation can be rather difficult, particularly when people don't know each other very well. A good way to get a conversation going is to ask questions. However, these questions must be of a *general* nature which your visitor can answer easily.

Topic	Questions and enquiries
Flight	*How was your flight?* *Did you have a good trip?*
Weather	*What was the weather like when you left London?* *What's the weather been like in England?*
Plans	*How long are you going to be here?* *How long are you planning to stay?*
Previous visits	*Is this your first visit to Germany?* *Have you been to Dusseldorf before?*
Visitor's town/country	*Which part of England are you from?* *Whereabouts in England do you live?*
Accommodation	*I hope everything is okay at the hotel.* *Where are you staying?*

PRACTICE 1 Now read the rest of Dialogue 1 and complete it with appropriate questions. When you have finished, check your version by listening to the cassette.

Dieter _____, Mr Dyson? Last time I was there we had beautiful clear days. Not like people think.

Richard *Rain, I'm afraid. Very dark. A lot of cloud.*

Dieter *Aaah. A more typically English day than I remember.*

Gerhard *If I can just ask you to wait here with Dieter, I'm going to bring the car round. I'll be just a minute or two.*

Dieter _____, Mr Dyson?

Richard *No, this is my first time. I was in Cologne a year ago, but I didn't come here. But I do like Germany, and in fact I've been to Hamburg several times. _____? You said you'd been to London.*

Dieter *Yes, but that was some time ago, when I was on holiday with my wife. And now London is quite expensive, I hear.*

Richard *I'm afraid so. Luckily, I don't live there.*

Dieter _____ then, Mr Dyson?

Richard *In a small town about 30 kilometres from the centre of London.*

PRACTICE 2 The following notes outline a conversation which takes place when Richard Dyson meets an ex-colleague of his. The two men used to work for the same company in the British and Italian subsidiaries respectively. They meet unexpectedly. Following these notes work out the details of the dialogue.

NOTES	**DIALOGUE**
Richard greets Francesco and comments that the meeting is unexpected.	*Hello Francesco. This is a pleasant surprise. Good to see you again. How are you?*
Francesco greets Richard and enquires about Richard's new job.	*I'm very well, but what about you? How are you? Are you enjoying your new job?*
Richard gives a favourable comment (interesting people). Then he asks Francesco why he is in London.	_____
Francesco explains it's a business trip (several meetings London/Milton Keynes for a few days).	_____

Richard checks his plans to find out when he's going back to Milan.

_____

Francesco says he will stay in London until end of week. Flight Friday a.m.

_____

Richard invites him for a meal at his home on Tuesday evening.

_____

Francesco thanks and accepts.

_____

Richard asks about his hotel.

_____

Compare your version with the key.

Francesco says the Strand Palace (very central).

_____

PART 2   CONVERSATIONS BEFORE MEETINGS

Background

Having spent the night at his hotel Richard Dyson has made his way to the German company. He is met at reception by Heidi Müller, a colleague of Mr Weiss.

Predicting the Conversation

What do you think Richard and Heidi will talk about on their way to Mr Weiss' office? Some subjects are suggested below. Say whether they are probable, possible or unsuitable at this stage of the conversation.

Speaker	Subjects	Probable	Possible	Unsuitable
Frau Müller	Details about Richard Dyson's job			X
	His business at the Germany company		X	
	His family			
	Previous trips to Düsseldorf			
	Travel to the company			
	Accommodation			
Mr Dyson	Type of products			
	Number of employees			
	Frau Muller's job			
	Turnover/profitability			
	Building			

Check your answers in the key.

Comprehension Check

Now listen to how Dialogue 2 developed and say whether the following statements are **true** or **false.**

1 Richard Dyson was expecting to meet Heidi Müller.

2 Heidi Müller expects that the hotel is satisfactory.

3 The company is a long way from the hotel.

4 Gerhard Weiss's office is in an old building.

5 In the past there were more employees than now.

6 Heidi Müller gives him some publicity material.

> Check your answers in the key.

Focus on Language

Listen to Dialogue 2 again and answer the questions below.

1 What does Richard Dyson say to show he is pleased with the hotel?

2 Heidi Müller apologizes because they have to walk quite a long way to get to Mr Weiss's office. What does she say to introduce the apology?

3 Heidi offers to take Mr Dyson to Mr Weiss's office. What does she say?

4 Heidi offers some company literature. What does she say?

> Check your answers in the key.

PRACTICE 3

You are working in Dallas. A colleague of yours, David Blair, has been delayed and has asked you to deal with a visitor until he arrives.

a Introduce yourself:

I'm _____ (name). *I work* _____ *Mr Blair.*

b Explain the situation:

_____ *Mr Blair has been delayed.*

c Offer him some refreshment:

Let _____.

d Ask him about previous visits to Dallas:

Is this _____?

e He's staying at the Grand Hotel. Check that everything is satisfactory:

I hope _____.

f You know the visitor is Brazilian but you don't know where he comes from:

Which part _____?

g Offer to show him round the department:

If _____.

PRACTICE 4   Terje Olson works for a Norwegian furniture manufacturer. He has been asked to take a Spanish visitor out to dinner. They have ordered their food and now keep the conversation moving by asking each other *general* questions.

Some of the questions they asked each other are given on the left. Match each question with the appropriate reply on the right.

a *How well do you know Oslo, Marcello?*

No, I come from the north originally. A small town up near the Arctic circle.

b *How's the Bristol? I've heard it's very good.*

Not at all. It's the first time I've been to Norway. In fact, it's the first time I've been in Scandinavia.

c *Do you have to travel a lot in your work, Terje?*

Very much. It's a beautiful setting and it's not as cold as I imagined.

d *Have you always lived in Oslo?*

Yes, it's fine. Very comfortable and the service is good too.

e *How are you enjoying your stay in Oslo?*

Yes, that's right. I've got a flat right in the centre.

f *Have you ever been to Spain?*

Not very much, a couple of times a year, mostly to the States.

g *You're from Madrid, aren't you?*

Yes, I was on holiday near Alicante last year. We enjoyed it very much.

PRACTICE 5   Now think of your own situation. If you were on business abroad, how would you respond to the following questions?

Remember to keep your replies to the actual questions as brief as possible, but add other related details or comments.

You're (your nationality) aren't you?

Where do you live?

Which part of (your country) are you from?

What do you do?

How long have you worked for (your company)?

Have you got a family?

Do you travel much in your job?

PRACTICE 6   Listen to the cassette. You will hear five instructions. After you have listened to each instruction, respond. You will hear a suggested answer after a pause.

> Check your answers in the key.

Key: Tapescript and answers

UNIT 1 TAPESCRIPTS AND ANSWERS

DIALOGUE 1

Guard	Good morning.
Guy	Good morning. My name is Guy Giradeaux. I've got an appointment with Mr Binder at ten.
Guard	Mr Binder. Sales Department?
Guy	That's right.
Guard	What was your name again?
Guy	Guy Giradeaux.
Guard	Okay, I'll phone through and tell him you're here.

DIALOGUE 2

Margareta	How do you do? I'm Margareta Sandström. I'm responsible for sales over here in the Stockholm area.
Guy	How do you do, Mrs Sandström? It's nice to meet you.
Margareta	Nice to meet you too.
Guy	So you have taken over from Björn Rendal?
Margareta	Yes, that's right. About two months ago, just after Björn left Le Saucier.

DIALOGUE 3

David	Mr Giradeaux?
Guy	Yes, that's right, Guy Giradeaux.
David	Hello, Guy, I'm David Fairlawn. Welcome to Daylight Electrics. It's great to have you with us.
Guy	Hello, David. Pleased to meet you.
David	Did you have any trouble getting here?
Guy	No, it ...

DIALOGUE 4

Terry	Georgina, you haven't met Ivan Chekov, the head of the Russian delegation, have you?
Georgina	No, not yet.
Terry	Well, come over and I'll introduce you. Interesting man.
Georgina	What exactly are they doing over here?
Terry	Something to do with a ferry for the Black Sea, I think.
Georgina	Really!
Terry	Hello, Mr Chekov. I hope you're enjoying the party.
Mr Chekov	Yes, very much.
Terry	Mr Chekov, I'd like you to meet a colleague of mine, Georgina Smiles from our design team.
Mr Chekov	How do you do?
Georgina	How do you do? I'm very pleased to meet you, Mr Chekov.

DIALOGUE 5

Terry	Hello, Patrick. If you've got a minute, there's someone I want you to meet.
Patrick	Certainly. Come in. I'll be with you in a moment. Right.
Terry	Patrick, this is Wolfgang Jaeger from Deutsche Lloyd. Patrick O'Connor, our Export Manager.
Patrick	Hello, Wolfgang. Nice to have you with us.
Wolfgang	How do you do?

DIALOGUE 6

Terry	Well, if everybody's here, let's begin. First of all, I'd like to welcome John Benny from the Chicago Consulting Group. As I'm sure everybody knows, the Chicago Consulting Group have been doing some market research for us, and Mr Benny is here today to give us their findings.
	John, let me introduce my colleagues from left to right: James O'Driscoll from R and D, Marion Flask, our financial expert, and Georgina Smiles, our design expert.

PRACTICE 6

1 Introduce John to a member of your family.

   John, this is my daughter Anna.

2 Introduce John to another guest who works for one of the big banks.

   John, I'd like you to meet Roger Herbert. Roger works for Central Bank. Roger, John Taylor, a colleague of mine from England.

3 Introduce John to another guest and her husband.
They are very good friends of yours.

*John, let me introduce you to two very good friends of
mine, Françoise and Roland Petit. John's over
from England for a few days.*

PART 1   INTRODUCING YOURSELF

Comprehension Check

1 No

2 a Dialogue 2
  b Dialogue 1
  c Dialogue 3

3 a Dialogue 3
  b Dialogue 2
  c Dialogue 1

Focus on Language

Dialogue 1   Task a   *I'm Guy Giradeaux.*

                 Task b   *I'm here to see Mr Binder.*

Dialogue 2   Task a   *My name is Margareta
Sandström.*

                           *I'm in charge of sales over here in the
Stockholm area.*

                 Task b   *I'm very pleased to meet you.*

Dialogue 3   Task a   *Are you Mr Giradeaux?*

                   Task b   *Hello, David. Nice to meet you.*

PRACTICE 1   **SUGGESTED ANSWERS**

a *Hello, my name is ... from Databloc. I've got an
appointment with Mr Bell at 10.30.*

b *Hello, I'm/My name is ... I'm here to see Mr Bell.*

c *Hello, let me introduce myself. I'm ... . I'm in charge
of/responsible for ...*

d *Hello, Mr Yamamoto, I'm/My name is ... from ... I'm
in charge of...*

PRACTICE 2   **b** *It's very nice to meet you at last.*

c *We're very pleased to have you with us.*

d *I'm very pleased to welcome you all here.*

e *I'm pleased to meet you.*

PRACTICE 3 **Dialogue A**

Donald You must be Janine Brown.

Janine Yes, that's right.

Donald Hello, I'm Donald Flinders. I'm pleased to meet you.

Janine Pleased to meet you too.

Dialogue B

Smallbone Are you Mr Francis, by any chance?

Francis Yes, that's me.

Smallbone I'm Clive Smallbone.

Francis Nice to meet you.

Smallbone I'm Head of Marketing here. You're from Databloc, aren't you?

Francis Yes, that's right.

PART 2 INTRODUCING OTHERS

Comprehension Check

1 a **Dialogue 4**
   b **Dialogue 6**
   c **Dialogue 5**

2 Ivan Chekov a the head of the Russian delegation
              b interesting man

   Wolfgang Jaeger from Deutsche Lloyd

   John Benny a from the Chicago Consulting Group
              b The Consulting Group has been doing some market research.
              c Mr Benny is here today to give us their findings.

Focus on Language

Dialogue 4 Task *May I introduce a colleague of mine?*

Dialogue 5 Task *May I introduce ...?*

Dialogue 6 Task *I'd like to introduce my colleagues ...*

PRACTICE 4 **SUGGESTED ANSWERS**

a *I'd like you to meet Tom de Wey, who is the Marketing Manager with our Dutch subsidiary.*

b *I want you to meet Francis Renard, a friend of mine from France.*

c *May I introduce Mr Utowa, who is the Sales Manager of one of our suppliers in Japan.*

PRACTICE 5   **SUGGESTED ANSWER**

Rita   Hello, David. How are you?

David   Fine, and you?

Rita   Very well, actually.

David   Have you met Peter Jennings, my new assistant, before? *or*
I don't think you've met Peter Jennings, my new assistant.

Rita   No, we haven't met.

David   Peter, may I/let me introduce Rita Vanders from OMU in
Holland.

PRACTICE 6   See the tapescript for Practice 6 on page 64 and 65 for
suggested introductions.

UNIT 2   TAPESCRIPTS AND ANSWERS

DIALOGUE 1

Tom   Morning, Mr Hamilton.

David   Hello, Tom. Everything okay?

Tom   Fine. By the way, I've finished that analysis of foreign sales
revenue. It's on your desk if you want to have a look at it.

DIALOGUE 2

David   Morning, Isabel. How are you?

Isabel   Oh, hello, Mr Hamilton. I'm fine. Terrible morning, isn't it?

David   Yes, and I forgot my umbrella. I'm soaked. Any messages?

DIALOGUE 3

David   Morning, Jane. You're in early. How was the holiday?

Jane   Oh, hello, David. Holiday? Just look at all this, it'll take days
to work through. No really, David, it was wonderful. Just what
I needed.

David   Sounds great.

Jane   How have things been here?

David   Fairly quiet. By the way, there's a departmental meeting this
afternoon, do you know about it?

PRACTICE 3   SITUATION A

David	Hello, Jan. How are you?
Jan	Fine, David, thank you. And you?
David	I'm okay. Now, what about ...

SITUATION B

Louise	Hello, Jane.
Jane	Hello, I'm not too late am I?
Louise	No, I only arrived a few minutes ago.
Jane	Let's order something to eat and then you must tell me about Greece. How are you enjoying life there?
Louise	Not much. To be honest with you the job's not that interesting and it's so hot.

SITUATION C

Mark	Hi, David, I'm over here.
David	Hello, Mark. You're back?
Mark	Yes, I got back this morning.
David	How was it?
Mark	Okay, I think, but it's hard to say. I'm never that optimistic until I get something down in writing.

SITUATION D

Francesco	Good morning, Mr Hamilton.
Mr Hamilton	Morning, Francesco. I haven't seen you for a while. I thought you must have left us.
Francesco	No, not yet. I'm not going home until the end of next month.
Mr Hamilton	And how have you been getting on?
Francesco	Very well. It's been a very useful few months and I've enjoyed being here.

SITUATION E

Maria	Hello, Isabel.
Isabel	Hello, Maria. I didn't know you were going to be here. How are things?
Maria	Great. I've got a really interesting new job.

SITUATION F

Pierre	Jane.
Jane	Hello, Pierre. Has your course finished?
Pierre	No, not yet. I've still got another week to go.

Jane	How's it going?
Pierre	Not too well. I'm a bit disappointed really.

DIALOGUE 4

David	Hello, Mr Inomata, I don't know if you remember me. David Hamilton, we met at ...
Mr Inomata	Of course! It's nice to meet you again, Mr Hamilton. You'd just moved over to Brussels when I was last there. It must be nearly 18 months ago.
David	That's right. Are you just over for this meeting?
Mr Inomata	No, actually, I'm over here for the Trade Fair.

DIALOGUE 5

Jacques	Hello, David.
David	Hello, Jacques. This is a pleasant surprise. I didn't know you were going to be here.
Jacques	Nor did I. Jean Grassi was due to come, but he couldn't manage it, so I'm here instead.
David	I see. Well, it's nice to see you again, Jacques, it's been a long time. How are things in Paris?
Jacques	Pretty good. The autumn was a bit slow, but things are looking up. And you, David. Are you still enjoying Brussels?
David	Yes, very much.

DIALOGUE 6

Sven	Hi, David.
David	Sven. Great to see you again. You're looking well.
Sven	Yes, I'm fine. A bit tired though. I just got back from the States yesterday.
David	Really. How did it go?
Sven	The trip?
David	Yes.
Sven	Interesting, not that I saw much, you know what business trips are like. But what about you and the family? I haven't seen you for well over six months. Are you all well?
David	Very well, actually ...

PRACTICE 6 1 You have just been introduced to an American visitor, Mr Clark. Greet him.

How do you do, Mr Clark? I'm very pleased to meet you.

2 You have just arrived at work. Greet a colleague of yours, Mary Oliver.

Good morning, Mary. How's everything?

3 A colleague of yours, Tony Ortiz, has just got back from a business trip. Greet him and enquire about the trip.

Hello, Tony. How was your trip to Brazil?

4 You are meeting Tom Grey at the airport. He is on a routine visit to your company. Greet him and enquire about the flight.

Hello, Tom. Nice to see you again. Did you have a good flight over?

5 You have just met an ex-colleague of yours, Jane Marsh. She was transferred to another department a few months ago, and you haven't seen her since then. Greet her and enquire about the new job.

Hello, Jane. I haven't seen you for a while. How's the new job going?

PART 1   DAILY GREETINGS

Comprehension Check

1 a Dialogue 3
  b Dialogue 1
  c Dialogue 2

2 Dialogue 3

3 a relaxed and friendly

4 Dialogues 1 and 2

NOTE

This is probably because his assistant and secretary are both much younger than he is. Usually first names would be used but sometimes as a sign of respect for age, titles and surnames are used.

Focus on Language

Dialogue 1   Task   *How's it going?*

Dialogue 2   Task   *Is everything all right?*

Dialogue 3   Task a   *How did you enjoy your holiday?*
            Task b   *Marvellous.*

PRACTICE 1   SUGGESTED ANSWERS

a *How was the flight/trip/journey?*

b *How was the film/movie?* or

How did you enjoy the film?

c *How did it go?* or
How was the trip?

d *How's your wife?* or
How's she doing?

e *How's the new job?* or
How's the new job going? or
How are you enjoying the new job?

PRACTICE 2 **b** *How are you enjoying life there?*

c *How was it?*

d *How have you been getting on?*

e *How are things?*

f *How's it going?*

PRACTICE 3

Enquiry	Positive	Negative	Actual reply
c		✔	*Okay, I think, but it's hard to say.*
d	✔		*Very well*
e	✔		*Great*
f		✔	*Not too well*

PART 2 GREETING PEOPLE YOU SEE LESS FREQUENTLY

Comprehension Check

1 a Dialogue 5

b Dialogues 4 and 6

2 a Approximately 18 months ago

b Some time ago

c Over six months ago

3 a Dialogue 4

b Dialogues 5 and 6

Focus on Language

Dialogue 4 Task *I'm pleased to meet you again.*

Dialogue 5 Task *It's good to see you again.*

Dialogue 6 Task *How was the trip?*

PRACTICE 4   SITUATION 1

  b *Good to see you again.*

  c *How's everything?*

  d *I'm sorry I've kept you waiting.*

  e *Let me give you a hand with your bags.*

  SITUATION 2

  b *I don't know if you remember me. I'm Philip Brooks. We met at ...*

  c *It's nice to meet you again.*

  d *How are you?*

PRACTICE 5   **SUGGESTED ANSWER**

Pierre Hello, David.

David Hello, Pierre. Good to see you again. It's been a long time. How's everything going?
   or
   Hello, Pierre. Nice to see you again. I haven't seen you since last year. How are things?

Pierre Okay. We've been extremely busy and it looks as if it's going to continue. What about you? I hear you've been transferred to headquarters. How's it going?
   or
   And yourself? I heard you got a new job yourself. How are you enjoying it?

David Okay, so far. Everything's going very smoothly and I'm enjoying the challenge.

PRACTICE 6 See the tapescript for Practice 6 on pages 69 and 70 for suggested greetings.

UNIT 3   TAPESCRIPTS AND ANSWERS

DIALOGUE 1

Emma I should be able to get most of the interviews done by the end of next month, and I'll try to get a report to you by early June, if that's all right with you.

Mr Martinez Yes, fine. Right then, that seems to be everything so I'll say goodbye and thank you. It's been a very useful meeting.

Emma Good. Well, goodbye Mr Martinez, I'll look forward to seeing you in a couple of months.

DIALOGUE 2

Tom	Are you having a coffee, Emma?
Emma	No thanks, Tom. I really must be going. I've got a client coming in at three and I want to look through his file.
Tom	Okay. See you later then. I hope everything goes well.
Emma	Thanks Tom, bye.

DIALOGUE 3

Brad	You must be really pleased. Things sure seem to be going well over here. Anyway, Emma, they're calling my flight so I'd better get going. I don't want to have to rush like last time.
Emma	Okay Brad, goodbye and have a good flight back.
Brad	Sure thing. I'll see you sometime in the fall and we can go through some ideas for next year.

DIALOGUE 4

Emma	Well, goodbye Dr Lenk. It's been very interesting talking to you. Thank you very much for giving up so much of your time.
Dr Lenk	That's all right, Mrs Sanderson. Goodbye. I'm sorry I couldn't be of more help.

DIALOGUE 5

Emma	Well, this is where I get off.
Passenger	Let me give you a hand with your case.
Emma	Thank you.
Passenger	Right, here you are. Have you got it?
Emma	Yes, thanks. So goodbye. I've enjoyed talking to you.
Passenger	Goodbye, and don't forget that restaurant I told you about. It's really very good.
Emma	I won't forget. Goodbye.

PRACTICE 7

1 You have just arrived in Paris by train. Say goodbye to another passenger, and say how much you've enjoyed talking to him.

Goodbye. I have enjoyed talking to you.

2 You have just taken an important visitor to the airport for his flight back to the States. Say goodbye and wish him a pleasant flight back.

So goodbye, Mr Abrahams. I hope you have a pleasant flight back.

3 You have been at a monthly international meeting. Say goodbye to an American colleague and refer to the next meeting.

Goodbye, Dan. I'll see you again next month.

4 You have been out for a meal with a friend. Say goodbye and thank him.

Bye, Dave, and thanks for the meal. It was very good.

5 It's Friday evening. Your assistant is about to leave for the weekend. Say goodbye and wish him a pleasant weekend.

Bye, and have a good weekend.

6 You've been visiting a company in Austria. Say goodbye and thank your host for organizing the visit for you.

Well goodbye, Mr Schmidt, and thank you for everything. It's been very interesting.

PART 1 CONCLUDING A CONVERSATION WITH PEOPLE YOU KNOW

Comprehension Check

1 a **Dialogue 2**

   b **Dialogue 3**

   c **Dialogue 1**

2 a **Dialogue 3**

   b **Dialogue 1**

   c **Dialogue 2**

3 **Dialogue 1**   in a couple of months

   Dialogue 2   later the same day

   Dialogue 3   in the fall/autumn

4 **Dialogue 1**   Mr Martinez

   Dialogue 2   Emma

   Dialogue 3   Brad

5 a **Dialogue 2**

   b **Dialogue 3**

   c **Dialogue 1**

Focus on Language

Dialogue 1 Task *about two months*

Dialogue 2 Task *I'm afraid I've got to go.*

Dialogue 3 Task *I'll say goodbye. Enjoy the flight.*

PRACTICE 1   **SUGGESTED ANSWERS**

a *Goodnight, Isabel. Have a good evening.*

b *Goodbye, Alain. I'll see you sometime next month.*

c *Goodbye, Mr Heinig and thank you for everything.*

d *Goodbye, Shaun. I hope you have a good flight back tomorrow.*

e *Goodbye, Mr King and we'll look forward to seeing you when you're next over here.*

PRACTICE 2   **SUGGESTED ANSWERS**

a *Goodbye, Anna. Thank you for all your help.*

b *Goodnight. I'll see you tomorrow/in the morning at nine.*

c *Goodbye, Jan. Have a good flight back and I'll see you next month in Denmark.*

PRACTICE 3   **SUGGESTED ANSWER**

Colleague   When are you leaving Ramon?

Ramon   In about half an hour. I want to get away before the traffic gets bad.

Colleague   Okay. Well, I'll say goodbye now and have a good holiday.

Ramon   I'm sure I will. I'm really looking forward to a month of good food and sun.

Colleague   I bet. Anyway, enjoy yourself and I'll see you when you get back.

PRACTICE 4   b *I think that's everything, Mr Fish.*

c *I really must go, Tom, or I'll miss my train.*

d *I really should be going, David.*

e *It's been a very nice afternoon, but ...*

PRACTICE 5   **SUGGESTED ANSWERS**

a *I really must be going. It's rather late and I've got to ...*

b *I really must be going. They're calling my flight.*

c *I really should be leaving. I've got a lot to do this afternoon.*

d *I think I really should be going. Thank you very much for an excellent meal/evening. or It's getting rather late and I'm afraid I have a meeting tomorrow morning.*

PART 2 CONCLUDING A CONVERSATION WITH PEOPLE YOU DON'T KNOW

Comprehension Check

1 **Dialogue 5**

2 **Dialogue 4** A laboratory supervisor, or someone in the research department.

Dialogue 5 Someone she meets by chance on the train.

3 **Dialogue 4**   by prior arrangement

Dialogue 5   by chance

PRACTICE 6

a *Goodbye. I've enjoyed meeting you.*
b *It's been nice talking to you.*
c *It's been nice meeting you.*

PRACTICE 7 See the tapescript for Practice 7 on pages 73 and 74 for suggested conclusions to the conversations.

UNIT 4 TAPESCRIPTS AND ANSWERS

DIALOGUE 1

Christina   Yes, I think we've covered most of the points.

Brian   Good. Are you going to be in London for a few days, Christina?

Christina   Yes, until the beginning of next week.

Brian   Well, er, my wife and I have invited some friends for dinner tomorrow and, if you haven't any plans, we were wondering if you'd like to come?

Christina   That's very kind of you, Brian. I'd be delighted to come.

DIALOGUE 2

Brian   How did you like the meal, Lars?

Lars   Oh, it was very good.

Brian   Well, if you like English cooking, would you like to have dinner at my house? Maybe sometime next week before you go back to Sweden.

Lars   Yes, that would be very nice, Brian. I'd like that very much.

DIALOGUE 3

John   So it's been a good day, Brian. I think we've sold nearly twenty of the B 2 11's.

Brian   Not bad for one day. Oh, John, some of us are going for a drink after the exhibition has finished. How about joining us?

John   Thanks. Good idea. Where shall we meet?

PRACTICE 1　　1 *My wife and I would like to invite you for a meal this week. Are you free?*

2 *John, can you come round for lunch on Saturday? We're having a few friends in.*

3 *We're going to the theatre on Saturday and we were wondering if you'd like to join us.*

4 *If you're free on Friday why not come round for a drink?*

5 *Would you like to look round the department on Thursday morning? I'm sure we could arrange it.*

6 *If you're going to be in Munich next month why don't you call in and see us? We'd be very pleased to see you.*

7 *If you haven't any plans this evening perhaps you'd like me to show you some of the town.*

8 *This is David Thompson's secretary. He would like to invite you to dinner next Friday. Would that be possible for you?*

DIALOGUE 4

Brian　So in a few days you'll be back in Paris, Jules.

Jules　No, tomorrow evening actually. I have changed my flight.

Brian　Oh, then, if you're free this evening perhaps you'd like to come round for a meal. Nothing special but ...

Jules　That's very kind of you, Brian, but I don't think I can. It's my last night and, well, I've still got a lot of work to do.

Brian　Well, maybe next time.

PRACTICE 5　　1 *A* If you're free this evening would you like to go out for a meal?
　　　　　　　　B Thank you very much, Tom, but I'm afraid I've already made arrangements for tonight.

2 *A* If you're not doing anything special why don't you come and spend the weekend with us?
　　B I'm afraid I don't think we can. One of the children is ill. Anyway, thanks for asking.

3 *A* We're having some people over for a barbecue on Saturday. Can you come?
　　B What a pity. We've got some friends staying all weekend.

4 *A* What about a quick drink on the way back?
　　B Thanks, Tom, but I really should get back to the office. I've got so much to do.

5 **A** Mr Johnstone asked me to phone you to see if you'd like to have lunch with him after the meeting on Thursday.

B That's very nice of him but I don't think I'll be able to. I've got to be in Frankfurt on Friday, so I'll have to get the train down on Thursday afternoon.

PRACTICE 7 **1** If you've nothing planned for this evening, my colleagues and I would like to invite you for dinner.

Thank you very much. That would be very nice.

2 If you're not doing anything special tonight, I was wondering if you would like to go to the theatre.

It's very kind of you to invite me, but I'm afraid I've already got something planned.

3 Jon and I are going to a football match on Saturday. Why don't you come?

Oh, what a pity. I don't think I can. We've got friends coming round.

4 Would you like to come over for a meal next Friday?

That's very kind of you. I'll look forward to it.

5 I don't know what you're doing tomorrow, but I'd be glad to show you round town.

Thanks very much. That would be very nice.

PART 1 INVITING AND ACCEPTING

Comprehension Check

1 **a** **Dialogue 3**
b **Dialogues 1 and 2**

2 **Dialogues 1 and 2** Dinner at his home

Dialogue 3 A drink

3 Accepted

4 **a** **Dialogue 3** (the language is rather informal)
b **Dialogues 1 and 2**

Focus on Language

Dialogue 1 Task *That's very nice of you. I'll look forward to it.*

Dialogue 2 Task a *Perhaps you'd like to have dinner at my house.*

Task b *Oh, thank you very much. I'll look forward to that.*

Dialogue 3   Task a   *Why don't you come?*

Task b   *Yes, that sounds good, thanks.*

PRACTICE 1

	Neutral	Informal	Expression
3	✓		*... we were wondering if you'd like to join us.*
4		✓	*... why not come round ...?*
5	✓		*Would you like to look round the department ...?*
6		✓	*... why don't you call in and see us?*
7	✓		*... perhaps you'd like me to show you some of the town.*
8	✓		*He would like to invite you ...*

See also the tapescript for Practice 1 on page 77.

PRACTICE 2   **SUGGESTED ANSWERS**

a *Would you like to go to the theatre tomorrow evening?* or

I have some tickets for the theatre tomorrow evening and I was wondering if you would like to go?

b *I was wondering if you would like to go out for a meal tonight.*

c *Why don't you come round this weekend for a drink?*

d *What about a game of tennis?* or

Why don't you join us for a game of tennis?

PRACTICE 3   **SUGGESTED ANSWERS**

a *Yes, Tom, thanks. That's a good idea.*

b *Yes, that's very kind of you. I'd like that very much.*

c *Yes, we'd like that very much. That's very kind of you/very nice of you.*

PRACTICE 4   **Dialogue A**

Brian   If you've nothing arranged this evening, Mr Vane, I was wondering if you'd like to come out for a meal with us.

Mr Vane   That's very kind of you. I'd like that very much.

Brian   Good. I'll pick you up at the hotel, about eight then.

Mr Vane   Fine. I'll look forward to it.

Dialogue B

Brian	I don't know what your plans are, Paul, but would you like to go out for a meal on Thursday evening?
Paul	Thanks very much. I'd love to.
Brian	Good. Shall I pick you up at the hotel?
Paul	Fine. About what time?
Brian	Shall we say half past seven?

PART 2 INVITING AND DECLINING

Comprehension Check

Dialogue 4

1 An invitation to dinner.
2 He's still got a lot of work to do.

PRACTICE 5

	Actual words used	Explanation
1	*Thank you very much... but I'm afraid...*	Other arrangements
2	*I'm afraid I don't think we can.*	Child ill
3	*What a pity.*	Visitors for the weekend
4	*Thanks... but I really should get back...*	Too much work
5	*That's very nice of of him. I don't think I'll be able to.*	Travelling to Frankfurt for an appointment

See also the tapescript for Practice 5 on pages 77 and 78.

PRACTICE 6 **SUGGESTED ANSWERS**

Dialogue A

Sven	Brian, look if you are not doing anything this evening/if you're free this evening, why don't we go out for a meal?
Brian	Thanks, Sven, but I'm already having dinner with Arne Brandsberg. What about tomorrow night?
Sven	Yes, that's fine for me. What time?

Dialogue B

Jan	Do you know Malmö at all, Brian?

Brian   No, this is my first visit.

Jan   Well, if you're not busy tonight, I was wondering if you'd like to meet me this evening. Then I can show you something of the town.

Brian   That's very kind of you but I'm afraid I've already arranged something else.

PRACTICE 7   See the tapescript for Practice 7 on page 78 for suggested ways to respond to invitations.

UNIT 5   TAPESCRIPTS AND ANSWERS

DIALOGUE 1

Frank   It's getting late, Philippe. I really should be getting back to the office.

Philippe   So should I. Well, many thanks for lunch, Frank. It really was very good.

Frank   Good, glad you enjoyed it. Next time we'll have to try to arrange to meet one evening.

Philippe   Fine, give me a ring and we can arrange a date nearer the time.

DIALOGUE 2

David   Did you enjoy the play, Philippe?

Philippe   Very much. I'm not sure I understood everything. My English isn't so good, but I got the general idea.

David   Good.

Philippe   Anyway, thank you for organizing the evening, David. It was an excellent choice.

David   I'm glad you enjoyed it, Philippe. It's had mixed reviews but last time you were here you said you like ...

DIALOGUE 3

Hostess   Have you enjoyed your weekend?

Philippe   Yes, it's been marvellous. It really was very kind of you to invite me. I hope it hasn't been too much trouble.

Hostess   Not at all. We've really enjoyed having you. I hope you'll come and stay again next time you're in Houston.

DIALOGUE 4

Mike   Here you are, Mr Blanchard. The view graphs you asked me to get ready for your presentation tomorrow.

Philippe	They look very good, Mike. Thank you very much. I hope it didn't take you too long.
Mike	No, really it wasn't any trouble. I did it one afternoon when I wasn't too busy.

DIALOGUE 5

Philippe	Excuse me, could you tell me where Dan Blair's office is?
Man	Dan Blair. Isn't he in the training section?
Philippe	Yes, that's right.
Man	Well, you're on the wrong floor. If you go up to the fifth floor, they'll be able to help you.
Philippe	Thank you very much.
Man	You're welcome.

DIALOGUE 6

Philippe	Can I have the key to room 238, please?
Receptionist	238?
Philippe	Yes.
Receptionist	Certainly. There's a message for you, Mr Blanchard. Here you are.
Philippe	Thank you very much.
Receptionist	Don't mention it.

PRACTICE 5

1 A   Thank you for letting me use your office.
   You   That's okay.

2 A   I did enjoy the meal. It was really excellent.
   You   Good. I'm glad you liked it.

3 A   It was very kind of you to invite me. It's been a very relaxing few days.
   You   We've enjoyed having you.

4 A   I think I've got all the details down. Thanks for the information.
   You   You're welcome.

5 A   Thank you for changing the flights. I'm sorry it was so complicated.
   You   Really, it was no trouble.

6 A   Thanks for the coffee.
   You   Don't mention it.

PART 1   THANKING PEOPLE FOR HOSPITALITY

Comprehension Check

1 **Dialogue 1**   at a restaurant

Dialogue 2   at/after the theatre

Dialogue 3   at his American host's house

2 **Dialogue 1**   lunch

Dialogue 2   a play

Dialogue 3   a weekend at his host's house.

3 **Dialogue 3**

Focus on Language

Dialogue 1   Task a   *It was a good lunch. Thanks for inviting me.*

Task b   *I enjoyed the meal very much* or *I have enjoyed the meal very much.*

Dialogue 2   Task   *It was very kind of you to organize the evening. It was a really good play.*

(The other choice is a little too formal.)

Dialogue 3   Task a   *Wonderful.*

Task b   *Thank you very much for all your hospitality. I really appreciate it.*

(The other choice is a little too informal.)

PRACTICE 1   **b** *It was very nice of you to invite me. I really enjoyed the play.*

c *Thank you for all your hospitality. I really have appreciated it.*

d *Thank you for getting me a ticket.*

e *Thank you very much for the meal.*

f *It was most kind of you to invite me over.*

PRACTICE 2   **b** *It was very funny.*

c *It's been a useful two months.*

d *It was a very exciting match.*

e *It was delicious.*

f *I've enjoyed myself a lot.*

PRACTICE 3   **SUGGESTED ANSWERS**

SITUATION 1

b *I really enjoyed the play.*

c *What a good choice!*

SITUATION 2

a *Thank you very much for inviting me.*
or
I really appreciate your hospitality.

b *You really have a lovely house/place.*

c *I've really enjoyed myself.*

SITUATION 3

a *The meal was delicious.*

b *It was very kind of you to invite me.*

c *I really like this restaurant/It's an excellent restaurant.*

PART 2   RESPONDING TO THANKS

Comprehension Check

1 **Dialogue 4**   Mike prepared him the view graphs.

Dialogue 5   He gets some directions.

Dialogue 6   He is given a message.

2 **a Dialogue 4**

b Dialogue 6

c Dialogue 5

3 **Dialogue 4**

PRACTICE 4   **SUGGESTED ANSWERS**

SITUATION 1   *You're welcome.*

SITUATION 2   *That's all right Mr Blanchard. Really, it was no trouble.*

SITUATION 3   *I'm glad you enjoyed it.*

SITUATION 4   *Don't mention it.*

PRACTICE 5   See the tapescript for Practice 5 on page 82 for suggested responses.

UNIT 6   TAPESCRIPTS AND ANSWERS

DIALOGUE 1

Helga   Do you know where I can borrow a car?

Bill   Hiring a car is terribly expensive. Why don't you borrow our second car? It's a VW and I expect you're used to driving one of those.

Helga   I'd really appreciate that, Bill. Are you sure you don't need it?

DIALOGUE 2

Helga   Well, thank you Mr Jeffery, I have enjoyed my visit to the branch, and now I've got a good idea about how you do things here.

Mr Jeffrey   I'm glad you found the visit useful, Mrs Müller. By the way, how are you getting back to town? Shall I order you a taxi?

Helga   Thank you, but it's not necessary. Mr Seeley has lent me a car for my stay – a Volkswagen.

DIALOGUE 3

Woman   Do you know, I've been looking for someone who could give me some information about sending my daughter to stay with a German family.

Helga   Well, I haven't got any children of school age, but my neighbours may be interested. Would you like me to give you their address?

Woman   Yes please, I'd be very grateful.

PRACTICE 3   Dialogue a

A   That's what I'm phoning about. I just wanted to check your travel arrangements. Have you fixed up a hotel?

B   Not yet.

A   Well. Do you want me to book you in somewhere?

B   No thanks, Tom. It's really not necessary. Our travel department does that kind of thing.

Dialogue b

A   So, I'll see you next Friday. What time are you arriving?

B   Well, my flight leaves just after 2. I should be in around 3.30 your time.

A   Do you want me to pick you up?

B   Thanks Ian, but really don't bother. I'll take the airport bus and we can meet sometime later in the evening.

Dialogue c

A   I'm afraid Mr Johnstone is going to be a few minutes late, so can I bring you something to drink?

B   Yes please, that would be very nice.

Dialogue d

A Do you know if it's possible to get tickets to the opera?

B I'm not sure but, if you like, I could try to find out for you.

A That's very kind of you.

DIALOGUE 4

Helga Excuse me, can you give me a hand? My car's broken down and I need to push it off the road.

Passer-by Sorry, I'm already late for a dental appointment. Try asking those two people behind me.

DIALOGUE 5

Helga Excuse me, could you possibly help me to push my car off the road? It's just broken down.

Passer-by Yes, of course. Where do you want it to go? By the way, I thought Volkswagens didn't break down.

PRACTICE 6 **Dialogue a**

A Excuse me, do you think I could have a quick look at your paper?

B Yes, of course. Here you are.

Dialogue b

A I need to change my flight back to San Francisco. Do you think you could arrange that for me?

B Certainly, I'll see what I can do.

Dialogue c

A I need some papers sent over from the States. Could you possibly contact my secretary and have her ring me here this afternoon?

B Yes, no problem. I'll get in touch with her straightaway.

Dialogue d

A I'd like to order something to eat.

B I'm very sorry but that's not possible. We don't serve after 9 p.m.

Dialogue e

A David, could you give Marion Bennet a message when she comes in?

B I'm afraid not. I'm going to be out of the office all afternoon.

PART 1   OFFERING

Comprehension Check

1   a   **Dialogue 3**
    b   **Dialogue 1**
    c   **Dialogue 2**

2   **Dialogue 1**   the loan of a car
    Dialogue 2   ordering a taxi
    Dialogue 3   an address of a neighbour

3   **Dialogue 1**   Accepted
    Dialogue 2   Declined
    Dialogue 3   Accepted

Focus on Language

Dialogue 1   Task   *How about borrowing our second car?*

Dialogue 2   Task   *That's very kind of you but no thank you.*

Dialogue 3   Task   *If you like, I could give you their address.*

PRACTICE 1   **SUGGESTED ANSWERS**

b   *Do you want a lift?*
c   *If you like, I could put some brochures in the post.*
d   *Can I get you all another drink?*
e   *Would you like me to book you a room in the local hotel?*

PRACTICE 2   **SUGGESTED ANSWERS**

a   *Let me take your coat.*
b   *Shall I get you/phone for some coffee?*
c   *Would you like to see some of our company literature?*
d   *If you like, I would be glad/happy to show you round the factory.*
e   *Let me know if there's anything else I can do/you would like.*

PRACTICE 3

Offer	Accepted	Declined	Expression
b pick up airport		✓	*Thanks, Ian but really don't bother.*
c a drink	✓		*Yes please, that would be very nice.*
d find out about tickets	✓		*That's very kind of you.*

PRACTICE 4   **SUGGESTED ANSWERS**

     a *That's very kind of you but I've already asked Mr ... to do it.*

     b *Thank you, but I'm going to order a taxi.*

     c *That's very kind of you but I'm going out tomorrow/I've already made other arrangements.*

PART 2   MAKING REQUESTS

Comprehension Check

     1 On the road – her car has broken down.

     2 Someone to help her push the car off the road.

     3 He's got a dental appointment.

PRACTICE 5   **SUGGESTED ANSWERS**

     a *Would it be possible to change the date of our meeting?*

     b *Could you call me a taxi?*
        Could you possibly call me a taxi?

     c *Do you think I could ring home?*
        Do you think I could possibly call home?

     d *Would it be possible for you to show Mr Weiss round the department?*

     e *Can you give me/let me have change for £1?*

PRACTICE 6

	Request	Negative	Positive	Expression
b	Change flight		✓	*Certainly, I'll see what I can do*
c	Contact secretary and ask her to ring		✓	*Yes, no problem*
d	Order food	✓		*I'm very sorry but that's not possible*
e	Give someone a message	✓		*I'm afraid not.*

PRACTICE 7   **SUGGESTED ANSWERS**

    a *I'm sorry, but I'm not wearing a watch.*
      I'm afraid not, I haven't got a watch on.

    b *Certainly. I'd be delighted to.*

    c *I'm afraid not. I have another meeting.*
      I'm afraid I can't. I've another meeting.

    d *I'm sorry, but I'm terribly busy.*
      I'm afraid not. I'm terribly busy.

UNIT 7   TAPESCRIPTS AND ANSWERS

DIALOGUE 1   *First part.*

Gerhard	Richard, it's good to see you again.
Richard	Hello, Gerhard. Thank you for meeting me.
Gerhard	Richard, I'd like you to meet my assistant, Dieter Brand. He's very interested in talking later about one or two of your products.
Richard	Pleased to meet you, Dieter.
Dieter	Very pleased to meet you, Mr Dyson. Did you have a good flight.
Richard	Not bad. A bit bumpy coming in to land, but not bad.
Gerhard	Next time you should try Lufthansa, Richard. So. Is this your luggage?
Richard	That's right. About those samples you wanted me to bring over. I've got them with me, except for the 356. I'm very sorry about it but we've been having trouble with our suppliers.
Gerhard	That's all right Richard. Now we have to walk a little. I have my car so there's no need for a taxi.
Richard	It's very kind of you, Gerhard but I really could have found my way into town myself.

PRACTICE 1   *Dialogue 1 continued*

Dieter   **How was the weather in London,** Mr Dyson? Last time
I was there we had beautiful clear days. Not like people
think.

Richard   Rain, I'm afraid. Very dark. A lot of cloud.

Dieter   Aaah. A more typically English day than I remember.

Gerhard   If I can just ask you to wait here with Dieter, I'm going to
bring the car round. I'll be just a minute or two.

Dieter   **Have you been to Düsseldorf before,** Mr Dyson?

Richard   No, this is my first time. I was in Cologne a year ago, but
I didn't come here. But I do like Germany, and in fact I've
been to Hamburg several times. **What about you?** You said
you've been to London.

Dieter   Yes, but that was some time ago, when I was on holiday.
With my wife. And now London is quite expensive, I hear.

Richard   I'm afraid so. Luckily, I don't live there.

Dieter   **Where do you live** then, Mr Dyson?

Richard   In a small town about 30 kilometres from the centre of
London.

DIALOGUE 2

Heidi   Mr Dyson? I'm Heidi Müller, Mr Weiss's personal
assistant.

Richard   Oh, good morning. Mr Weiss told me you would meet me.

Heidi   So, I hope everything is okay at your hotel? It's a new hotel
and we have put quite a few visitors there this year.

Richard   Yes, it's very comfortable. Very convenient for the centre,
and quite close to your company too.

Heidi   So you had no difficulty coming here? Did you come by
taxi?

Richard   No, I walked. The weather is quite good and I like the
exercise.

Heidi   Well, I'm afraid we still have quite a long walk to Mr
Weiss's office, Mr Dyson. I hope you don't mind.

Richard   No, not at all. Are we going now?

Heidi   Yes, if you'll follow me. I'll take you there.

Richard   The building seems very new. When was it built?

Heidi   Well, this particular building was put up in 1983. Before
that we were outside the centre, on the other side of the
river.

Richard   And how many people are here now? I mean how many
employees are there here?

Heidi	On this site we have nearly two thousand, but we have another seven hundred or so in Stuttgart.
Richard	Does that mean the number of employees has dropped? I thought that ...
Heidi	Yes, it has. A typical story. But as you probably know, after the restructuring of the company last year we have actually increased the number of divisions to four.
Richard	Yes, I was reading about that in some publicity material.
Heidi	Well, if you'd like to have more details, I can let you have the company report. Ah. We take the lift here.

PRACTICE 6

1 You have been asked to meet a visitor, a Mr Blair, at the station. Ask him about the journey.

Did you have a good journey, Mr Blair?

2 You have to welcome a visitor, a Mrs Francis, prior to a meeting. Greet her and ask her if she had any problem finding her way.

Good morning, Mrs Francis. Did you have any difficulty finding your way here?

3 You are in a restaurant in Paris with a visitor to the company. You have just finished the meal. He is leaving tomorrow after a week's visit. Ask him if he has enjoyed his stay.

I hope you've enjoyed your stay in Paris?

4 You are meeting a visitor at reception. You booked the hotel for him.

How do you like the hotel?

5 You have been introduced to someone at a party. Ask about this person's job.

What kind of business are you in?

PART 1 CONVERSATIONS WHEN MEETING PEOPLE

Predicting the Conversation

The conversation *might* well include the following: the flight, the weather, the hotel, the tape samples, previous visits to Dusseldorf, in addition to greetings.

Comprehension Check

1 False 2 True 3 False 4 False 5 False

Focus on Language

1 *It's good to see you again.*

2 *Thank you for meeting me.*

3 *Richard, I'd like you to meet my assistant, Dieter Brand.*

4 *I'm very sorry about it but we've been having trouble with our suppliers.*

5 *It's very kind of you, Gerhard.*

PRACTICE 1 See the tapescript on page 90 for the complete dialogue.

PRACTICE 2 **SUGGESTED ANSWERS**

Richard Very much. I've met a lot of interesting people. So, what brings you to London?/So, what are you doing in London?

Francesco Well, I'm here on business for a few days. I've got quite a few meetings here in London and in Milton Keynes.

Richard And when are you returning to Milan?

Francesco Well, I'm going to be/stay in London till the end of the week. My flight's on Friday morning.

Richard Well, if you're not doing anything on Tuesday evening, would you like to come over for a meal?

Francesco Thank you very much. I'd love to.

Richard Good. What about your hotel? Is everything all right? Where are you staying?

Francesco I'm staying at the Strand Palace. It's very central and …

PART 2 CONVERSATIONS BEFORE MEETINGS

PREDICTING THE CONVERSATIONS **SUGGESTED ANSWERS**

Speaker	Subjects	Probable	Possible	Unsuitable
Frau Müller	Details about Richard's job			x
	His business at the German company		x	
	His family			x
	Previous trips to Düsseldorf	x		
	Travel to the company	x		
	Accommodation	x		

Mr Dyson	Type of Products		X	
	Number of Employees	X		
	Frau Müller's job		X	
	Turnover/Profitability			X
	Building	X		

Comprehension Check

1 True 2 True 3 False 4 False 5 True
6 False (she only offers it at this stage)

Focus on Language

1 *It's very comfortable. Very convenient for the centre, and quite close to your company, too.*

2 *Well, I'm afraid we still have quite a long walk to Mr Weiss's office.*

3 *If you'll follow me, I'll take you there.*

4 *If you'd like to have more details, I can let you have the company report.*

PRACTICE 3 SUGGESTED ANSWERS

a *I'm John Smith. I work with Mr Blair.*

b *I'm afraid that Mr Blair has been delayed.*

c *Let me get you some coffee* (or other suitable drink).

d *Is this your first visit to Dallas?*

e *I hope everything is fine with the hotel. (Okay/all right).*

f *Which part of Brazil do you come from?/Which part of Brazil are you from?*

g *If you like I'll show you round the department.*

PRACTICE 4

b *Yes, it's fine. Very ...*

c *Not very much, a couple of times a year ...*

d *No, I come from the north originally ...*

e *Very much. It's a beautiful ...*

f *Yes, I was on holiday near Alicante ...*

g *Yes, that's right. I've got ...*

PRACTICE 5 SUGGESTED ANSWERS

Yes, that's right. I come from ...

In a small town ...

From the (north ...)

I'm an engineer ... I work in the area of ...

For about six years. I was in ... before.

Yes, I have. I've got a boy and three girls.
Quite a lot/Not much/Two or three weeks a year.

PRACTICE 6   See the tapescript on page 91 for suggested responses.